MW00612319

13.95

Mule Tracks:
The Last of The Story

HOWARD COPENHAVER
Author of "They Left Their Tracks"

Mule Tracks:
The Last of The Story

Howard Copenhaver
Author of "They Left Their Tracks"

Copyright 2001 by Howard Copenhaver

Published in the United States of America

Library of Congress Number 2001096121

Second Printing, January 2004
First Printing, October 2001

ISBN 1-931291-14-4 (Softcover)
ISBN 1-931291-15-2 (Hardcover)

ALL RIGHTS RESERVED
No part of this publication may be reproduced, stored in a retrieval system, or transmitted in any form or by any means without the prior written permission of the copyright owner or the publisher.

STONEYDALE PRESS PUBLISHING COMPANY
523 Main Street • P.O. Box 188
Stevensville, Montana 59870
Phone: 406-777-2729
E-mail Address: stoneydale@montana.com
Website: www.stoneydale.com

Table of Contents

COVER PHOTO – *One of the more famous photographs taken in Howard Copenhaver's hunting camp in the Bob Marshall Wilderness over the years shows one of his pack mules and Walter Pelzer, taxidermist for the Milwaukee, Wisconsin, Museum, hamming it up for the camera. Pelzer and others from Milwaukee were in Montana to collect mountain goat specimen for the museum and the mules' dependable work in the wilderness was the subject of an article in the Milwaukee Journal by writer Mel Ellis in October of 1956. This photo of Pelzer, now deceased, and the mule appeared in the Journal as part of that story.*

Figure This Out

Men who work their life with these hard tailed long ears find out at an early age it's not only men who can think and plan. These mountain canary's some time have a faster and long lasting brain. They never forget a foul trick or one to their benefit. This all brings to mind a poem written by a lover of mules a long time ago.

I can't remember all the words but thought here is the place for what I can remember.

"THE MULE SKINNER"
Old mule you are the son of a jackass
And I am the image of God
Yet here we work hitched together
Just a tillin' and tollin' the sod
Soon the plantin' will be over
Next when the harvest is done
That crop will be split three ways
One-third for me, and one-third for you,
And one-third for the Landlord's pay
Now you take your one-third
And eat it, seems you're getting
The best somehow.
I spent my one-third between a wife
Eight kids and a cow
Don't 'peer to me this is even
And set me to wonderin'
Who is the Mule and who is the
Goddamn Fool?

ILLUSTRATIONS – *The artistic work of four individuals grace the pages of "Mule Tracks: The Last of The Story." They are Bill Ohrmann, J. Rangitsch, Howie Fly and Anthony Lapka, who also happens to be Howard Copenhaver's grandson. The illustration above is by Howie Fly and relates to the story on Page 44.*

Foreword

If one has paid any attention to the flow of Howard Copenhaver's storytelling methods over the years, and I think I have, three factors rise dominant above any others when you consider what he's out to accomplish when he shares a tale out of the wilderness with you. The first is that he's talking right at you, to you the individual, a person, his friend, a fellow confidante in the story he's relating. Wherever he might be physically, in his storytelling mode he's right across the campfire from you, deep in the Bob Marshall Wilderness, late in the evening with a fire flickering and a pot of coffee warming in the space between you and a good, hard day that you've shared with each other unifying your purpose for being there. When Howard shares a story with you, whether it's orally around the wilderness campfire or in a big city auditorium, he's put you and your enjoyment of the story front and center.

Second, the subject of a particular story might seem mundane to some but to Howard, and to you his audience, it becomes monumentally central to the significance of life itself. In many instances, all of us realize that his stories touch basic elements of our own experiences in the wild. Thus, his vitality, in either spoken or written words, becomes our vitality, our comprehension of and involvement in the episode he relates in direct relationship to a mutual comprehension of what life in the wild is all about.

And third, he invariably casts the characters in his stories in a light that we can respect them whether they're good, bad, or otherwise, human or wild or simply such incomprehensible a creature as the mule.

Howard Copenhaver enjoys international renown as a storyteller of the first rank. He regales in the process of sharing the episodes of his life in the wilderness, even when he's the butt of one of his stories, and readily admits that some of the wildest places he's ever seen go by the name of New York and Washington and Chicago, and so on. Even today, at eighty-seven, he's more at home deep in the forested wilderness of the Bob Marshall, that vast million-acre enclave of the majestic elk and the noble grizzly bear, than he is in the confines of the big city. And yet he also readily admits that he often wishes he'd kept a journal of his many experiences because, as a natural storyteller, he has to rely on the power of memory to bring out of his subconscious mind the details of the stories that, when he was closer in time to them years ago, lay in recession there.

He spoke of this difficulty when writing his third book, "Copenhaver Country," where he followed the advice of a good friend and spent a lot of time "back-tracking" over old trails to summon up the details that put life and vitality into his stories. In the process, he says he came to realize that in his earlier books he'd only delved into a few of the many stories in which his beloved mules were central to the wilderness experience and he wanted to write more about them.

Constant among the requests that have come to Howard over the years from those who have enjoyed his books are that he do something special about mules, particularly since he speaks so highly of this incredible critter in his writings. So, he's put together a book in which the mule and the tracks in the wilderness they've made alongside Howard's are central. "Mule Tracks: The Last of The Story" includes Howard's observations about the mule as dependable pack stock as well as their universal reputation for being contrary creatures. Some of his mules, and in particular the legendary Patches and his famous bell mare, Black Moll, are elevated to superstar status, even sainthood if you believe in that sort of thing for pack mules. Most of his mules performed their task as pack stock in anonymity. Others were, well, just contrary, or funny, or bewildered, sometimes stubborn, or what-have-you. Whatever the case, they were never boring.

Howard emphasizes in his stories that, most often, the mules that came to him for training and inclusion in his wilderness pack strings were rough stock that needed quick training so they could be used right away. Thus, the techniques he developed and used were keyed to the necessity of getting things done quickly and thoroughly. One couldn't take a chance in the wilds, with hazardous trails and such coincidental incidents as occasional encounters with grizzly bears, with stock that was only half-trained or undependable.

Howard also realized, however, that he had some unsaid and unwritten memories to share about another episode in which he played a central role, that of taking his pack string of mules into the canyons of many eastern U.S. cities, and in particular Washington, D.C., and New York as part of the Montana Centennial Train in 1964 when it was a major part of the World Fair being held in New York that year. Thus, "Mule Tracks: The Last of The Story" also includes a few tales involving Howard and his mules in that setting – including the incredible Patches The Queen and her masterful, and superior, handling of her journey into that, to her at least, strange and extraordinary place. Like everything else she did, Patches seems to have handled that forced-upon-her experience just like she handled life in the wilderness, right in stride and with grace and great acumen. You can't read about Patches without coming to love her.

However, like the master storyteller he is, Howard not only shares numerous stories involving his mules from out of the past but also brings us to the present, to his own adjustments with changing factors in his own life – sometimes downright funny, as he's prone to be, and sometimes downright profound. His new book ranks with "They Left Their Tracks" for both its clarity and the profound joy that Howard finds in everything he encounters, and does. And like he did in his earlier books, he makes sure you're either along for the ride or sitting at that campfire with him. Enjoy!

Dale A. Burk
Stevensville, Montana
September 30, 2001

MEETING HOWARD
on the Big Slide

Introduction

I know, I know. I'm just a bit different. Not stupid, just unintelligent.

But I can't understand these editors and literature-minded people. Just when you get to writing good they say, "That's two sentences or you got to have chapter here." Why? I've sat and listened to the best story tellers of all time and I've never seen them stop for periods or stop and say, "Hey Fellows, Chapter Three," and then go on with their tale. I think you should finish what you got to say.

So, I just sort of rattle on and you can make your own chapters. Sometimes I get the cart in front of the horse but he don't mind, why should I?

Howard Copenhaver
Ovando, Montana
September 18, 2001

This illustration by Howie Fly relates to a story on Page 43 and involved a mule named Bobby and a cook named Dutch.

Part One

*M*ules *played a major role in Howard Copenhaver's life as an outfitter*

in the famous back country of Montana's Bob Marshall Wilderness. They've also played a major role in his storytelling over the years. Whether it was working mules, training them or sharing their often hilarious antics, Howard always admired these critters, who demonstrated daily that they merit their fame for having a mind of their own. Thus, it is perfectly natural that the mesh so intimately with his tales of adventure in the wilds of Montana.

Howard was, however, a practical man, an outfitter, who used mules in mountain conditions, even dangerous circumstances, where their steadfastness was a necessity. That he knew how to prepare mules for that task is beyond question. And that he considers his beloved mules not only up to the task but generally superior to horses as pack stock, is also a given; otherwise he wouldn't have persisted in their use over the decades that he outfitted in the Bob Marshall Wilderness. In this section of the book, Howard shares a few humorous stories about his mules. He also outlines, as a recognized master, a number of tips on training and working mules, on doing the things that make them into the dependable back country pack stock they are..

You also find stories about other aspects of life in the wilds that helped shape Howard's attitude, experiences that gave him the wondrous "twinkle in the eye" of a born storyteller.

Howard and Marg Copenhaver in Ovando, Montana, in a picture taken in October of 2001.

Chapter One

The Last of the Story

I am sitting here on a high ridge, thinking of what I've done with my life and what mebby I should have done. When you look back over 86 years of mules, horses, and the miles they've followed you, there's a hell of a lot of thinking can be done. Lots of laughs and some crying with mixed tears and sweat. Don't help to cry. I've tried it and bellyaching only makes things worse. So, you laugh and bear it.

I've rode horses and dragged those long ears where no other man has done it. Tell you what, you find one and I'll buy the drinks at the next stop.

From here, I look out over Pintler Wilderness, the Flint Creek Valley, north to the Bob Marshall Wilderness, Scapegoat Wilderness, then north to the Great Bear Wilderness, the Mission Range to the west, farther southwest to the great Bitterroot Range, north and west to the fabulous St. Joe River of Idaho.

Now, there's Cooper Lake Range with Daley Peak and Mineral Mountain hiding the Continental Divide, but there's Old Red Mountain sticking her head high above all as if she can't be left out of the picture. Have I been there? Yes, and those long eared hard tails right behind me. If there is game, fish, fires and scenery, we've been there with a dog close behind.

In 1964, they also followed me up and down the main streets of fourteen major cities from Missoula, Montana, and Billings, Montana, to those fourteen cities east of the Grand Old Mississippi River. Right up Pennsylvania Avenue to the front door of the Capital in District of Columbia, greeted by Senator Mike Mansfield and President Lyndon Johnson.

What a pack trip! Excitement? You bet your last buck we had it. That little gal of mine right beside me – spurs, chaps, and saddle. Not one bellyache, just a frown once in a while – she doesn't approve of my vocabulary.

In my memories, my first experiences with these hay burners was when I was a small boy. My brother and I were standing in the barn door feeding hands full of grain to some big old Percheron work horses. It felt so funny, them licking grain off your hands with those big soft lips. Guess we weren't feeding them fast enough because one of them stepped his big Number 10 foot up on the step where my foot was. Where my toenail went, I don't know. But, how it felt, I sure react. I can feel it to this day and that toenail is thick as a chunk of sole leather, and just as hard. Makes me ouch just to write about it – mebby this is where I gained those impressive words.

When I was seven or eight years old, I was driving four head, harrowing plowed ground to make it smooth for seeding wheat. I walked behind the harrow and drove four abreast. Over the many years that followed learning how to handle teams, then on to riding, breaking them as colts, and packing them, I've picked up much knowledge from many old boys who'd already been there and shared their knowledge with a button.

When I was young, horses were the main mode of travel and power. Finally, mules were brought into our country, used mostly as pack stock with far better luck then horses. Good mules have far more and better ability as pack stock than horses. Their surefootedness, and abilities to carry heavy loads in rough mountain trails and work in a string are far better than horses. They also stick together in a bunch much better, not so many loners.

I'd rather pack the sorriest mule than the best horse in a string. Once you're loaded, all you need is miles and he'll come around.

Pinkie The Mule

This mule was a snake I got when I bought twenty-two in one bunch and was gentled as I will explain further through this story.

Now my first real experience in packing was tending sheep camp in summer range in the mountains. It was moving camp and getting supplies to a sheep herder summering a band in the Cooper Lake Mountain range rough country. My brother, Gene, and I moved camp from place to place as the sheep fed off the feed.

For pack animals, Dad gave us two big Percheron work horses, very gentle. Mike and Pat were their names. He also built four big wood boxes which we hung one on each side of the horse. They had open tops. We were too small to lift the heavy boxes when loaded so one of us would climb up on the horse sitting on his rump. Then, the other would throw up the supplies and pack them in the boxes until we were loaded. You had to balance the weight in each one. When we went a ways and the heaviest box would tip the saddle to one side, we'd pick up rocks and throw them up onto the light side. Didn't make any difference to Pat and Mike, they were big and stout.

Well, I suppose I better tell you how to start your mules and horses so's they'll stick in one bunch when you turn them loose to graze in the mountains. Sure ruffles a guy's hair to get up in the morning and find no mules or no bells ringing off on a hillside, just tracks to follow.

Like an "old boy" told me one time, he always had the skinniest stock I ever saw in the hills. I says to him, "Why don't you turn them ponies loose and let them graze." He says, "They can eat when I get home. D'ruther see hide and bones in the morning than tracks on the trail." Guess he had something there but I sure didn't need any of it.

There ain't much use of me telling you just part of it if I'm going to help you. So, I'll try to explain what worked for me. Most was handed down by old-timers still rubbing spots with linament that were bruised as they learned the lesson. I'll start by how to shape up these hay burners so's they'll stay together and you'll not have ten head in twenty bunches in five different counties.

Difference in breaking horses years ago as compared to year 2000.

If some people saw us Old Boys handling these green horses years ago, they would call the Humane Society right off. Things were much different back then. Number one you did not have green horses or mules raised in a patio or ranch who were used to people. They were raised on big ranches in large numbers. From the time these colts were foaled they run on open range. Usually in the roughest pasture land and are gathered and altered and branded then kicked back to the hills till they are two to three years old. Some slip by at round up and may be six or more years old before they came up for sale. So you might say they are as wild as elk or deer they run with.

All of our other stock was in the mountains on pack trips. A dude ranch down the river had these three old saddle mares they wanted to sell as they were too old to stand hard work so we bought them. These kids didn't care how old they were. Just so's they were horses and they could ride them. We didn't plan to use them other than this week. They did a good job with the kids as they sort of took care of them no pain or worry. Just put the kids on them and let them go.

At this time three big three-year-old steers got out into another ranch and I had to go find them and bring them home. All the saddle stock I had was a rank colt and these old nags. I saddled up this colt and caught up the strongest looking old mare and a guy at the ranch rode her.

We found these steers about five miles away shaded up in a thorn brush thicket fighting flies. Every time I'd get them out in open country this one steer would cut back into the brush. This lad helping me was hopeless as a cowboy and I knew he could not ride the colt I was on. So I says, "Give me your horse and you just stand here and hold this colt." My plan of attack was I take the old mare and tie my catch rope solid to the horn then rope this steer and step off leaving the horse and steer to fight it out. I was sure the steer would jerk her down as he was big strong and wild. Well, she caught this steer and I started to sly off just as the rope hit the end. Now years ago some cowboy had trained this old girl as a rope horse. She ain't forgot nothin'. When that steer hit the end of that rope she screwed her tail in the ground and set the brakes, me, I'm halfway off and in the air when she stopped and dropped her reins and set her hind feet her shoulder came up, hitting me with the back of the saddle. End over end I go staking out a claim on the North Forty. Now as I've said once you get the knowledge through that skull good they'll never forget it. Horse or mule. Never stop half way. I'm afraid this goes for people also.

Now there was another element that enters into this outfitting no one except an outfitter would understand. When you book some guest you better have enough stock to seat them all. They don't like to walk.

It so happened that this one year we were full to the top. When we gathered our stock from western pasture, what did we find? Fourteen saddle mares, all of them with spanking new baby colts. Now what to do, we're short seven saddle horses? If we can find them they'll cost up more money than we've got and mebby half spoiled. In the home pasture we have seven three year old colts ready to be broken to ride and only three weeks till we had to set people on them. There is only one thing we can do. Get out our saddle and start into ride. I called up and old friend, Ted, and told him my sad tale. He says, "Let's get started," so we did.

These colts were not real wild but half hot blood and snakey. We put them through their training I'm about to explain and in three weeks we sat those people on them and they rode them ponies for seven weeks over hill and dale and ten-day pack trips through the Bob Marshall Wilderness and not one person ever had any trouble.

In other words you can't spend four months to a year petting and gentling a colt for saddle if you are to stay in business. These same horses we used until Father Time swung his scythe all of them good.

When you start some colts or brought some new stock and hauled them home, they're lonesome for friends and their home range. Horses and mules

are not loners; they like friends. I pick an older mare who is cranky (or a gelding). Mares are the best; bell mares, usually. You put her in a small corral with your new stock. Feed them hay and leave them together for a few days. She'll kick and bite them, but, before you know it, they'll fall in love with her and follow her all over the place. Mules seem to fall in love easier and never forget it. They're a bunch of lonely doves. They like a leader. Usually, four or five days does the trick and will save you many an hour or days looking for them. It also pays big to take your colts along on the trip. They learn how to behave and get around in the hills. Now in the mountains, you have different forage than at home and they have to learn to eat other vegetation by watching the older horses and mules. We usually take them at two years old with a light pack so's they know the complete story.

Next comes breaking them to pack saddle and halter so's they will lead up and keep in a line. This is a must or you're in trouble. This is with young stuff that has not been handled before. I don't like old stuff as they usually

have learned bad habits and manners that are hard to break. They pick up tricks that are bad and dangerous.

Don't be rough on them. Make them respect and like you from the start. Give them a hand-out of oats. People say oats make them wild. I say oats are the best gentler ever grown; all horses and mules like it. Just like candy to a kid.

I can be as tough as any mule and still not be abusive. They're just like a child. You have to have respect from them and show them respect so's they'll look to you for help when needed. The best way to gain respect is, have a good foot rope and also a ketch rope, and learn how to use them right.

You tie a bowline around their neck, back around a hind foot, give your rope a twist. Then, back up to the loop around his neck running the loose end through the loop. When you pull, it lifts the hind foot off the ground. Let it clear the ground by four inches. He'll fight and fall, but stand up again. He only needs three legs to stand on. Bring your rope back round the foot below the ankle, wrap it once, then back to the loop around his neck, tie it off with a slip knot so's you can jerk it loose if you want to turn his foot loose.

Now you can work all around him. He can't kick or strike. And, they learn right sudden who's the boss man. Rub their ears, face, neck and back. Even give them a handful of grain out of your hand. You'd be surprised how the smell of oats takes the fear and spook out of them. Use this a number of times. If they throw themselves and won't get up, you just tie all four feet in a bunch and let them lay there in the hot sun. When they start braying, go over and pet them, get them up, but don't turn that hind foot loose till he stands quiet on all three. It don't take long to get it through their thick skull who's boss and you can help them. Mules learn quick and remember. You'll have to do this several times but it works. Never get too trusting; they're just animals.

Mebby I should keep my mouth shut and not bother you with how I like to buy and train mules but I think I ought to. Might help you or someone else. It's worked great for me.

Tell you what, I only had one mule that didn't respond to this treatment. She was a beautiful black Molly, five years old, and this guy says, "No man can gentle that mule." Well me, I think I can, so I gave him $35.00 for her and went to work with her. She was just like a wild animal; plumb crazy. We packed her and after she was loaded and tied in the string, worked perfect, but when you either packed her or unpacked her, you tied up a hind foot and hobbled her front. Sometimes, I tied her fronts to a tree or she'd kill you. We were on a long trip one summer and figured every day for three weeks would soften her up, but no deal. She only got worse. Now, we're over on the Sun River Game Range and only three days left on the trip. When we wrangled one morning, she was gone. We searched for her all day and packed up and left for the ranch the next day. Still no mule. Later that winter, when the elk migrated out to the winter range, people called me and said they kept seeing a black mule running with the elk. I says, "I already lost $35.00 and had no bruises, so why go get her. If she liked those elk, let her stay there." Reports kept filtering back to me from the winter range for several years. Guess she died of old age, but, undoubtedly, happy.

Well, on with my story. I like to go into a bunch of young ones and pick my own. I'll walk in through them. The ones that spook and get out of my way the fastest, I buy. If they show a lot of spook and fire, that's just what I'm looking for. A snakey mule will gentle faster than a more gentle acting one. They are smart and will mind their own business and not get into trouble. Once you have a handle on them, they're good for life and respect you and what you teach them. A mule always takes care of himself first and he thinks.

I take them home and put them in a pen with a bell mare as I said before. When I'm satisfied with this lesson, I rope each one several times, never dragging on the rope, just pull his head to point your way. Turn him loose and do this until when you walk up toward him, he'll spin and look at you. It takes time but not as much as patching up a wreck on the trail or chasing him around a corral for an hour trying to get a halter on him so's you can go to work.

Talking about rank stock making hands out of me and my brother reminds me of an old friend, Hubert Hunt. Now I've seen some rope hands in my day – guys that when they picked up a plain old rope in their hands it just seemed to some alive not just a coil of entangled twine. He was the best. I was just a kid trying to learn.

We were in a corral full of horses and I was trying to lay a loop on a horse I needed. He'd ducked my loop three or four times when Hubert says to me, "Let me see your rope." He took it and built a small loop and hung it over his left shoulder. Then he walked in a half circle paced the horse and kegged up in the end of the corral. As he went by there they dashed one by one past him to the other end of the pen. When the horse I wanted made his dash, Old Hubert flipped that loop off his shoulder and out in front of that pony running along the corral fence. That loop stood up on edge and that pony stuck his head in that loop. Hubert set his feet and held the rope across his hips, stopping the horse in a sudden jerk and he led right out of the bunch. Slick as a whistle.

Well, we spent the rest of the day roping horses, showing me the many tricks of his trade. I'll tell you my respect for age sure went up a notch that day. Now these are not rope tricks to astound people. They are the real necessities of roping horses or cows. I practiced till I got pretty handy and used this under handed back cast a lot. Especially in a corral. When you swing a loop around it stirs up your stock. If you use a hoolihan or pack cast you don't get them excited.

When it came to fancy stuff he could show you that too. One I always liked to watch him do was to make a big loop then lay it on the ground and twist it into a figure eight, fold it over like a sandwich and pick it up. It looked like a coil of rope in his hand. Then as a horse ran by him, he'd give it a flip out in front of this nag, give a jerk, and he'd have both front feet in a loop with a cross between them, dumping that old pony on his nose.

He would build a loop about two feet across and snap it out flat just once the heads of the horses and it would settle down over the head of one he wanted in the middle of the bunch. So smooth and easy, this became my favorite loop for horses.

One day I says, "Hubert, how did you learn to rope this way?" Well kid, it's a long story. All over eastern Montana and southern Canada, they built straw sheds for protection for stock in summer as well as winter. They would set a bunch of post about 10 feet high in the ground either in a circle or generally square. Then stretch woven wire around and over the top supported by barbed wire underneath to act as rafters. When harvest time came and they threshed the grain they'd blow the straw over the wire and post leaving an open entrance on each side. Some of these straw sheds were very large after a few years and when stock got in there it was warm.

Well there were lots of horses running the range at that time and would shade up in there in the summer and also in the winter get out of the storm. So when we were looking for horse we always hit the straw sheds. Our rider would block the entrance on one side and the other on the other side. If you saw a horse you wanted you'd build a small loop and flip it in over their heads laying it flat because you only had two feet or three at the most above the horses backs. After enough misses and practice you either got good at it or you done a lot of walking. Now cowboys don't like walking so I guess practice paid the bill. Especially when the horse you were roping belonged to someone else is the way he put it.

Handling a ketch rope takes practice but if you're going to work rank stock you better learn how.

After this, out comes my foot rope and up goes that left hind foot. He'll fight it for a while and then give up and stand still and look at you. You walk up to him, place your hand on his forehead, and scratch his face and ears, then back along his neck and back. Also rub his side and flank. Sure he'll fight and try to get away but keep after him. He'll give up. Then walk around, pet and scratch him on both sides talking to him all the time. If you're tired and cranky, cuss him if you want, he don't know what you're saying but he'll get used to your voice and listen for it when you come around. Sort of a tranquilizer (you hope). I 'm not kidding you, they'll learn to pick your voice out of others and pay attention to you.

Get your saddle (no blanket) and take after him; he'll fight that foot rope, mebby fall down, but he'll get up. You keep after him, let him smell the saddle, all the time telling him how nice you are or how good he is. Remember the tone of your voice has a lot to do with this schooling. Don't scream at him; he'll take offense and fear from your harsh, loud voice. Slide the saddle up his shoulder and onto his back. Sure, he'll jump out from under it, but keep after him. He'll soon let you lay it on his back. Next do it from the other side. Every time he stands, give him a handful of oats. I also like horse pellets. They like them and you can carry them in your pocket.

Never put the britching over his rump or cinch him up till he's completely accepting the saddle. At any point through this stage, don't take the foot rope off. They connect a rope around a foot as "don't move." You got the idea, well, so will the mule. Rub his face, ears, and neck till you can slip a halter on. Don't try to lead him; that all comes later. Just drop the lead rope to the ground. After he's got this through his skull and is half decent about it, give him a good feed of oats. Never work a colt or mule till he gets tired and mad. Make him seat up good but you can tell when he's had enough for a day. I like to work them in the morning, give them a rest, and then in the afternoon.

Running W

While I'm so strong on foot ropes I should tell you about another one.

Back when all the field work was done with hay burners and horse drawn machinery, the "Running W ("double you"), was a real necessity. Why? Because every rancher had a head of mebby up to fifty or more work stock. Now these were all big draft horses. Percheron, Clyde and Belgian. Weighing 1,500 to over 2,000 pounds. And most of them only worked twenty or so days in a year. Most in haying time. Then they were turned out on the range and were really never completely broke to drive and get gentle, but come haying time we used them anyway. Lots of time you changed teams at noon. Worked long hours and fast to beat the weather and

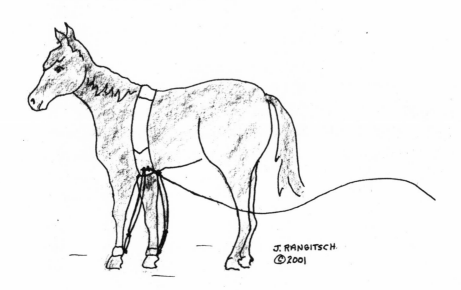

J. RANGITSCH.
©2001

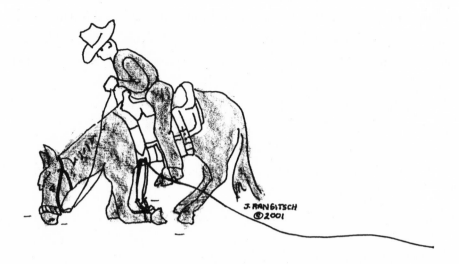

covered a lot of ground to get the hay up for the cattle in the long winters. If a horse got sore shoulders or a bad neck you'd run in another to take his place. Teamsters came from all over the West and Canada during haying season and they knew how to drive and get those old ponies to work. Now from lack of steady work these horse were never completely broke to be gentle to work stock. Lots of them became runaways.

If you were in a place where you could see a whole hay field you might see three or four runaways at the same time. This is where the "Running Double U" came in handy, and my friend, it was used.

You'd put a belt around the horse's girth (where you'd cinch a saddle). There was a rope fastened to the belt there running down to the inside ankle where a strap with a ring was fastened around the ankle, then back up to the belt run threw a small pulley, then down to the outside ankle threw another ring fastened to the ankle, back up to a ring on the belt then the rope ran back to the driver, he held this rope in his hand. When the horses took off too fast he'd jerk on his rope pulling the front feet up to the horses belly. The old pony's nose would hit the ground to a sudden stop. When you let slack in the rope Old Dobbin could get up and walk and go about the business of getting the haying done.

Some of these horses would run away every time you would just tie a string around their ankle tight before you started they'd work all day with out a hobble.

We had one team that we bought from a neighbor that were terrible runaways. Gene and me took them on a wagon out in a plowed field one day. Put the Running W on them and would let them run till they got up good speed then dump them on their nose. He replowed that field with their noses a couple of times. When we were done they got the idea that "Whoa" meant "stop." From then till they died if you hitched them to a wagon or a sleigh and before you started out would take your hand and squeeze it around their ankles they'd work all day just fine but if you just hooked them up and started out you could bet it would be a runaway. A man just could not hold those big 16 hand, ton horses.

These same runaways were just as nice and gentle as a dog but were spoiled from the start. When you start a horse or mule, don't stop half way.

The Running W – K. Price

Just the other day I ran into an old friend right near my age. He, just like his dad, was born in Blackfoot City, a ghost town today and many years before. Blackfoot City was also the birth place of Calamity Jane of western fame over the whole West and mebby the world. The city, a small cow country town, sets right up on top of the Continental Divide on the head of Snow Shoe Creek in the Avon and Nevada Country. It was a cow country and mining district in the 1800's. Cow country today.

Kenny Price's father was born up there in the spring of 1876. He became a cowboy rancher and horse man. He knew every trick of the trade when it came to rough horses and riding them.

Now after getting married he has this son, Kenny, who is following right in his father's tracks. One day they happened to ride into Avon and stopped at the store where a group of ranchers and cowboys were discussing a horse owned by one of the ranchers. It seems every bronc rider in the area had taken a seat on this old pony's back and all of them had lost even to the tune of a few broken bones and many bruises. Kenny and his Dad stood there taking it all in. When Dad says, "Why he don't look that bad to me. You know what? This fourteen-year-old kid of mine can ride him just like a D."

"Boy did my mouth fly open," says Kenny. "I can't ride him Pop." "The hell you can't," says Dad, "How much if he breaks him to ride?" "He can have him if he rides him. I'm going to kill him if someone don't get him rode."

Well Kenny and Dad head home with the horse, Kenny dumbfounded. Pops keeps saying, "Don't worry, you'll ride him sure nuff."

Next day Pops forefoot this horse and puts what he called a "Running W" on him then a flank rope around his flanks, hands me this long rope and says, "When I let him up you jerk on that rope, it'll tighten up around his flanks and make him buck." Pops lets him up and I jerk on the rope. Boy did he go bucking and kicking around the corral. Now when he got to going good Dad would pull on that Running W and he'd land on his nose in a big pile. Up he'd come and I'd jerk my flank rope around the show'd start again. Now it was fun for a while I was getting more tired than the horse, Dad says, "Don't stop till he does. Then keep jerking on that rope." This went all afternoon until finally he'd had enough and just stood there.

Dad took off the ropes and turned him loose. Next morning this old pony is sure stiff and sore. Dad catches him and throws my saddle on him and says, "Climb on." I rode him around the corral a couple of times real slow. He couldn't go any faster. He was sure nuff stiffened up. Dad opens the gate and says, "See the top of that mountain? Push him up there and then come back." Now it was late in the afternoon when we made the top of that mountain, but he was walking real good by then. By the time we got home he was traveling good. We used him for years and he never caused any trouble or bucked again. Now you asked me did I ever use a W. It sure works especially on work horses.

Now if you see Old Kenny Price walking along the street in Helena, Montana, after one look you'll know by him by the hitchin' he's got along and the bend of those knees that it was horse hair and leather that shaped them that a way. Not a four wheeler and gas fumes that today's' ranchers have to worry about.

Thank you Kenny for the story.

Now, back to your training. Be sure you treat the mule to his reward of oats. Soon he'll look forward to it and it all connects together in a ball between those long ears. Now tomorrow, we're going to give him his first lesson in a pack of weight on his back. You'll find going through this saddling and handling won't be so hard next day. (Don't forget the foot rope.)

After you've got your Decker pack saddle on him, take down your sling ropes and get two old truck tires. You tie the top of your tire to the back D

Ring and on the saddle hang so's it clears the ground about four inches. Then, with the sling rope, tie the back of the tire to the britching ring. Do this on both sides. Now he's got his first pack on. Take off your foot rope and let him have it all to himself. Leave his head loose, dragging the halter rope.

He'll put on a rodeo all by himself; usually kicks his feet through those tires and has the weight hanging on each leg. He can't get rid of those tires and soon he's on the ground. Let him lay there. Can't hurt himself, but he'll try. I like a hot sunny day as it sure cooks them laying on the hot ground. Soon, they'll lift their heads and look to you for help. I wait for them to bray or a horse to whinny. They're asking for help. Go and take your time talking to them, undo the tires, and let them up. Pet them and reload them. If they won't run away this time, take a rope and drive them around the corral, stopping and walking up to them each time.

A mule seldom hits the ground more than twice; a horse ain't so smart. He'll sometimes need the course several times, but it's all worth the trouble. Leaving the halter rope dragging gives you a way to show him you can catch him anyway and he should get used to ropes around his legs and feet. Now tomorrow, we'll put him in the string and show him how to lead once and for all.

Now this old long ear is finding out life is not all sunshine and grass. I like to work five or six at the same time because they find out getting run into and over isn't too much fun, roses, and sunshine. You catch them, tie up a foot, and saddle them the same way. Now comes the packs. I still use truck tires, only tie the front tight to the front; then run your sling rope back through the rear; tie it hard and fast. Thread your sling rope through your cinch ring around the bottom of the tire and cinch her down tight to your ring. Tie it solid and do up the end of the sling rope on the saddle front ring. Put the other tire on the other side. Now you have them all packed. Anchor one to a post and tie the next to his pig tail. Each halter has two lead ropes on it. Run the right halter rope through the britching ring and up to your pig tail. Do this on both left and right side, leaving enough slack in the halter rope so's the back mule has three feet between the front one. Tie the next to the last until you have a string of mules. Then tie your lead mule to the caboose mule or last one and turn them loose. If you have to give them a start, use a rope or blanket to spook them off center. Once they start, there'll be plenty of dust and mules trying to get away but it won't take long till they'll be following each other in a circle. When they stop, make them move out. I keep this up for several hours. Then, let them have it to themselves. Finally, one will stop and the rest will be glad he did and they'll stand in a circle.

I leave them for half a day all alone. They really get acquainted that way. Every once in a while one will decide it's time to go and everybody leads someone else. Don't do no good to pull back and they'll end up standing quiet with their heads down in the shade of the other.

Have good stout lead ropes and halters as they'll sure put the big test on it for stoutness.

After you unpack them, give them a good shot of oats, talking to them all the time. If one is goosey about eating oats, make him eat some out of your hand. Once he gets a taste, your troubles are over.

Lead in your bell mare or lead horse. After saddling and packing the tires on those hard tails, tie your lead mule to your bell mare with two lead ropes the same as you've done with the mules. Be sure to remember to always tie each mule in the same place in line. Why? Because each mule or horse has his own smell and the mule will get used to it and always follow the leader's butt. I've seen them so set in following another or having another mule behind them, that they'll kick a strange one behind them. Or if a strange horse or mule is in front, they'll bite and eat on them causing a lot of trouble. Also, they learn the stride of the mule in front of them and walk and lead with no jerking on their lead rope and become bosom buddies. Now this is just what you want to hold your stock together in one big bunch. No strays or loners to worry about.

Old Black Moll

In talking about one animal learning the smell of another and the stride of their walk, you should always tie your mules in the same place in a string. Just like 1-2-3 as they learn their place and who is in front of them for reasons I've already mentioned.

To explain I should tell you about "Old Black Moll" the best bell mare I ever owned. She was a half Morgan and over the fence Mare Dame with Cayuse and Percheron blood lines, making her a Dukes mixture of pedigree. But the best. She was cranky as an Old Maid school teacher but knew her job and always there near camp at home or in strange country.

Many's the time in the hills when having a lay over day we might have a later breakfast and we'd hear that days booming bell ringing and someone would say, "Guess 'Old Black Moll' thinks we should move." You'd go take a look and here she'd be coming into camp with all her mules strung out behind here. Each one in his own spot in line, just as if they were tied together.

When on winter pasture I've seen them all strung out in a line traveling around a mountain side headed for water, each in his own place and Moll in the head just like they knew what they were doing.

You can't train stock to do this but consistency sure pays off. They are animals of habit and don't forget it.

Pick up your lead mare's rope and circle the corral. Have someone open the gate after you have them lining out to suit you. I usually have a man ride along to help me if I have trouble. Head for the timber – small stuff, if you've got it, no trail, but right through the brush. If one gets his nose around a sapling, keep going. It'll bend and his nose will pop around it. If he starts around a large tree, the lead mare's butt will pull his head away from the tree as she swings it over to get around the tree herself. This is why you run two leads through the britching ring on each mule. The next mule will be pulled over by the one in front of him and so on down the line. When you get home, you might have to put some salve on a few skinned noses but the skin grows back quick and they have learned a valuable lesson.

Your mules will learn to keep their nose right on the one in fronts tail. It ain't no fun blazing a trail with their nose.

If you have only big trees, lead your string in a figure eight pattern around those big ones. The bell mare's butt will pull their head away from the tree as she swings around and so on down the line. He'll get so he watches for that swing giving him a cue as to where to go. Have luck, it surely has worked for me.

Another is training your saddle horse to lead a string. Some are good at it and some never make it. First, you teach your horse to stand ground hitched by just dropping your reins to the ground. Then, you take him and the mules into a corral. Stand them face to face. Tie the mule to your saddle horn with his head almost touching the horse's head and tie him to your mules pack saddle running both lead through the check of the others halter or bridle. Drop your saddle horses reins on the ground. Now their heads are tied together. When the mule wants to go, he bumps heads with the horse. Soon, the horse gets enough and starts biting him when he wants to pass. Bumping heads gets old quick and soon your saddle horse won't let nobody by him on a trail.

When you have to fix a pack on a trail and nothing to tie to spin your horse to meet your oncoming string, tie them together like so and your horse won't let them go by. I've had horses that every time you stopped them, they've spun around facing the other way even with no string behind them. Work, sure it takes work, but so does a wreck re-packing a string of mules because they won't stand still while you re-pack one down the line.

My motto in the mountains is be prepared and ready for anything. Tomorrow is a damn long way off, sometimes. Also, don't forget to pack a lunch.

If a mule jerks away from you, don't chase after him. He's a lonesome dove and he'll come back nine times out of ten and keg up with your string. Then you can pussyfoot around and get a hold of his lead rope and anchor him to another animal or tree. If you go running after him and he gets spooked, you'll have a long run.

Tom & Flashlight

This paragraph needs explanation, I believe. I got a late start from camp this day and ended up in the early darkness of evening. It was a twenty-nine mile trip and I had eleven head of long-ears loaded.

When I hit the McDermick Creek flats above Cooper Lake it was dark heavy lodgepole timber on both sides of the trail. As I crossed the creek and made a turn right in front of me is a string of pack animals in the trail. Suddenly I saw a dim light out in the timber. I holler, "Do you need help?" Back comes an answer, "You may help me catch this blankity blank colt." It's Old T.A. He's an ex-professor, sharp as a razor, but just never was long on good horse sense.

Seems this colt he was packing he'd tied on the tail end of the string. Always put a colt between two gentle ones. Well, the colt broke loose and T.A. had spent the afternoon chasing him around in the timber. It got dark and T.A. got his flashlight out. Every time he got close to the colt, he'd turn on the light to see the lead rope and away'd go the colt. I said, "T.A., get on your horse and head down the trail, stop at the first clearing and tie up your string and the colt will follow." He did this and when the colt thought he was being left he comes out of the brush and follows along behind. When T.A. stops to tie up his string, the colt crowds right up in to the middle of his buddies. I step off my horse, pussy foot around his gentle stock and get my hands on the colt's dragging lead rope and anchor him to the tail pack horse and holler a, "T.A. head for home."

Everybody is happy. T.A. says, "I've been chasing that damn colt since five o'clock till you came along." Horses and mules like company, the longer you chase them, the more scared they'll get, and chase them long enough and they'll just quit the country. Better to use your head than legs.

How To Keep Them Home

Another little trick a guy showed me was say you're up in rough high country where there is plenty of grass in a small place and you need to camp all night.

*TIE CLOSE SO
REAR MULE'S NOSE
JUST REACHES
THE GROUND.*

Now you know these ole hay burners are going to look for better country and grass. You take your lead horse and hobble her, then tail your mule to her leaving just enough slack so's he can reach the ground. Then tie the next one to his tail, then another to that one. Turn your lead horse loose. Now these nags are tired and hungry. The lead one will start to feed, so will the others. The one in front will lead the others around, they don't have room enough to step over the lead rope. When they raise their head to step it lifts the lead rope up and their feet are in the clear. Your lead horse will go to get a drink and so will the others. Most usually in such a case you will have two or three you can just turn loose and they'll stick as long as the leaders are there.

I have left six or seven of them this way for as long as two days and nights with no trouble.

The Forest Service used to send a young ranger along with our large parties using their stock. Well, Forest Service stock have only one idea in their head – go home.

I took care of them this way and never had to look for them again come daylight.

An outfitter's manual is just like a sheepherder's Bible, it's full of don'ts and you better learn them first. Always carry a foot rope on your bell mare. There is nothing needed more and as handy to have right handy, even with a solid gentle string. Whether it be used to doctor or shoe a mule, or tie up a foot for any reason.

Pasture

Well I've tried to explain a lot about this outfitting business and hope you enjoy it. The thing I have not touched on is these old ponies have to eat. They don't carry a lunch so it's your problem to get it for them.

Each country or state seems to be a bit different. Montana's Northwest and Continental valleys are, I guess, unique. While Wyoming, Colorado and parts of Northeastern Idaho have high plateaus, Montana's wildernesses have very fertile valleys and lush grass of many different kinds for feed, also with open hills of bunch grass, Idaho fescue, and broom grass, all excellent feed. Most outfitters just Bell their stock and turn them loose to graze at night. In Wyoming most hobble their stock. Here you have miles of open plateaus that stock can spread for miles away from camp at night, so hobbles are a must.

In Montana their grass land is surrounded by timber with lots of streams for water and they don't roam so far.

We have lots of grass and bushes they like, I've seen mules and horses raise their heads up and look at you when they look like they are picking flowers, there's so many different colors sticking out of their mouth. I've also looked back when going through a patch of bitter brush and see those old long ears with bitter brush branches half inch thick sticking out both sides of their mouth. Oh yeah, then you just hit a good huckleberry patch. Those old mules noses will be plumb purple in a short while. They'll walk along and grab a bush and eat it leaves and all on the go.

If you use hobbles put one on every animal. If you hobble only one or two of those that are free will travel and your hobbled stock try to keep up and before long you have sore legs rubbed raw by the hobbles or a hobbled animal all by himself you've got to look far. I've also seen this happen where a guy only hobbles one or two in a bunch. You go out to wrangle in the morning and jump the loose horses they head for camp on a run. This old pony with the hobbles takes after them as fast as he can jump along, sticks a hind foot over the hobble turns a flip flop and breaks his back. Not very often but I've seen it happen.

Another thing don't turn a horse or mule loose with a halter on or a rope dragging unless you are right there to watch him. One summer at Big Prairie I found three saddle horses that had been turned loose haltered that, scratching for flies, had hooked the halter under the heel of their rear shoe and broke their own necks fighting. When a horse is feeding in timber and down fall logs, a dragging lead rope is suicide, can get caught on a log. A horse that is tied in the timber is hard to find. This happens several times a year in the country I've worked all my life. Hope you can see the folly of these two practices.

Now, my friend, I didn't dream these tricks up. I watched old-timers and asked foolish questions. Some were answered and on some, I just got a grin. These old boys were the best of horsemen and mule skinners.

Bill Bell of the Forest Service Remount was probably the top mule man of his day and many more who worked their lifetime with horses and mules before the gas buggy replaced old Dobbins' life as the main way of transportation and freighting power.

I am sure they developed these tricks because of the many bruises and broken bones before they learned them.

Oh, yeah, another little one you might like if you have a colt that sulks up and won't move. Get yourself a harness ring about 1 1/4 inches inches in diameter, and pop it down over his ear lobe. He'll stand there and shake his head a bit then off he'll go. He'll forget his troubles and respond to your ideas. It works. If you could see my old saddle, you'd find a ring tied to a saddle string. I used it a lot. It's easy to use. All you have to do is lean forward in your saddle and pop it over his ear and head for home. Don't even have to get off.

Another technique is to work a colt after dark with a gas lantern in the corral. He can see nothing but you and will pay attention. With no outside attractions to get spooked at, he'll learn a lot faster. Just be sure to turn out the light before you go to bed.

Here's another I learned from Shorty Freeman, a top cutting horse trainer of his day. He put many a cutting horse to champions across the country, including Del Jay Hollywood and Hollywood Gold. Both were national champions.

Every horse has a different nervous system. Some are really high strung and hard to manage. Shorty showed me his stock of bits he used, about forty, all with different amounts of copper on the mouthpiece. He says he hangs a bridle on a colt with a bit of copper on it and turns the horse loose to eat hay. He watches the horse as the horse slobbers enough to suit Shorty. That's the bit he uses. Now he's changing that bit as this pony eats till his mouth has the right amount of moisture in it. What makes a horse so nervous, he claims, is that the mouth gets dry, causing the face to ache and nerve the horse up. He claims it also works with a mare in heat. She needs lots of copper in her mouth to calm her down. Most mares in heat are cranky and nervous.

I know that copper will do more than jerking the reins and a lead rope. This all comes by asking questions and as a kid, I had lots of questions and lucked out on answers. I guess it pays to be nosy and observing at the same time. Thanks Shorty.

Can you stand another one? Here is old Bill Ball again. This is how to halter break stock two years old and older. It also works on colts at weaning time if you choose to use it. Colts are small and you can handle them, but two and older are a little hard to handle by hand.

Bill had two big posts planted in the ground about 100 feet apart with a 5/8 inch cable stretched between them with ropes tied to it every nine feet or ten feet apart, with a ring on the lower end of the rope. He'd run these mules in the chute and put a halter on them. Then, with a big stout saddle horse, he'd drag them out under this high line. Throw them and tie all four feet together. We'd run their halter rope through the rings and lift their heads up about three feet off the ground. When we had ten of them tied to the high line, we'd turn their feet loose and let them up. I mean, they'd come off the ground headed everywhere at once. But, every time one hit the end of his rope, he'd jerk the next one over backwards and another one would jerk the next one back. What a bunch of dust and mules jerking each other this way and that. If one fell, he'd get jerked back up and he'd try to run away. Every time one sat back on the rope, he'd jerk another forward. You just sat and watched the circus. In a few hours, they had halter broke each other.

The best way is to do it just before dark and leave them there all night. Next morning, you can lead any of them with a twine string and no pull-backs. It sure puts the whoa on them and takes the sand out of their craw. We broke sixty-four of them snaky ridge-runners in five days. They were two years old and ran on the winter pasture for two years. Wild as elk and just as tough. I've used it on colts and it sure works good. Thank you, Bill, it's been a big help.

Now, another one – say you guys who's got a pull pack old pony breaking halter ropes and reins – run your lead rope over the hitch rail and back and tie it to her front ankle. When he hauls back, he'll jerk his foot up and slap himself under the chin. Sure puts the stop on some of them. If it don't work, a guaranteed way is to shoot the sun of a buck. Now, if you do this, be careful not to hit your halter. It costs money.

Well, you know where I come from and some of my background. I'll go on with where we've been and things that happened along the way. It's been a great life with lots of ups and downs.

By the way, I've mentioned how smart a mule is and not told you why. Guess I better do it.

Smart Mules

When I get into a jaw-swinging argument about smart horses and mules, my first question to my horse-loving friend is, "How many wire cut mules have you seen?" "I mean, mules with wire cut scars on their buttocks and legs. Notice all the scars at a horse sale more than any other place." This usually stops the argument.

I've seen unbroken mules standing in a pasture all alone – the rest of the stock, long gone. I go to see what's wrong with this long ear and here he's caught in an old barb wire fence laying in the tall grass or brush. One foot with a loop of wire around it. He's standing there holding his foot up. Now, when he first hit that wire, the barbs have scratched or cut the hide, but did he jerk and fight it? No, it hurt, and a mule will not hurt himself. He might kick at you or dance around, but never pull on the entangled foot. You cut the wire loose with lots of sweat and blow all threats. When he feels that foot is loose, he's gone like a bullet. Don't even say thanks!

I've seen them laying flat on the ground, all tangled up in wire. This happens when they're running and hit wire and fall. But, when those barbs start to stick through that skin, they say, "Better take care of me, nobody else will."

Now, a horse just plain loses his sense and goes hog wild. I've seen them fight it till they cut half way through a heavy leg bone.

By the way, the best thing I've ever found for a bad wire cut is to clean it up with soapy water. Air dry it. Then, pack it full of bucket honey. Rub it up the leg high above the wound. (No bandage, please.) Then turn him loose out to pasture. Give him six weeks or two months and that honey will heal it up, sometimes with very little scar tissue. Honey seals it so no flies or dirt can get into it.

We had this mule we could not keep in a corral at all. He was always getting out. The fence was six and a half feet high so he wasn't jumping out. All the other stock mules and horses never got out, but every morning, Jasper was on the outside by himself. One night, I sat out there and watched. After dark, he'd walk around smelling the ground close to the fence. When he found a spot he liked, he'd paw along the ground under the pole on the bottom of the fence. When he pawed long enough, he laid down with his back to the fence, right up close. Then, wiggle his neck and shoulders under the rail. When his head and neck were well under, he'd start kicking his hind feet, forcing his body under the rail till he could roll up on his belly. This forced the pole to bend up and he'd stand up and go off grazing around the yard.

The other stock inside would walk around the corral wanting out and smash down all the sign he'd left where he pawed the hole under. I'm sure he did not plan the last of part of hiding the evidence, but who showed him how to get out, if he couldn't think?

Then, there was Blackjack and Maggie, two skinny black mules that really had a love affair. They were always right together, not over fifty feet apart even when grazing on the hill. They started quitting us when we were in the hills and head for the home ranch, leaving us with their saddles to pack out and short two pack mules.

We were going to can them, but I came up needing them real bad on a big, long trip so's I took them in. They done just fine the first four days, but when we camped at Salmon Forks on the Flathead River, things changed. When the boys wrangled the next morning, Blackjack and Maggie were gone. I'd just finished breakfast and said to old Ted, "Fetch up Red and I'll go get them." I know they'd head for the ranch up river four days away. I took a shortcut and, by riding hard and fast, when I crossed the river at Murphy Flats and hit the main trail, there were no mule tracks in the dust. I knew I was ahead of them so I rested my horse and waited, watching down across White River Park. This is a big flat bench land a mile and a half long – all open except for some huge big yellow pine over one hundred feet tall. Along about noon, I sees my black friends come up out of the brush along the river and heading my way. I shook a loop in my ketch rope and parked out of sight. When they got good and close, I turned old 'Red' loose after them and dump my loop on Maggie – sets old Red up and lays Maggie flat on the ground with a big flop. She gets up and leads right up to me. I gets off Red and ties a bowline around her neck. Blackjack comes right up and I tie the other end of my rope around his neck. Gets back on Red and starts them down the trail for camp. They start to spread out and I drops that rope and holler, "Whoa!" You should have seen them go. Me, I'm right behind, and cut Maggie off around a big pine tree. When those long ears hit that tree, one on either side at a dead run. When the rope between them hit that tree, they both stopped, about five feet off the ground and came to a sudden halt, flat on their sides. Sort of knocked the air out of them. They got up and just stood there with their heads low and shaking them.

I got them straightened out and down river we go. They try to split again and I take after Blackjack. He goes around another big tree and we stretched them out again just as hard. This time, they get up a little slower and I line them down the river to camp again. Now old Maggie says, "I'm going to camp," and she took off down the trail on a run. Blackjack drops right in behind, stepped over the rope they're tied together with, and does a flip-flop, dumping Maggie also. When they get up this time, they hit the trail for camp. Blackjack keeps that rope snug but is running all the time, three and a half miles to camp and right up to the corral and the rest of the stock. We packed them all over the Bob Marshall for years and they never quit us again. Are they smart, or just forgot the way home?

Oh, yeah, then there was Bobby. She could get into more trouble and get out of it without getting caught up to, than you can imagine.

One time, we were camped on the bench on White River with a fishing party. It was a frosty summer morning. I had just wrangled the stock and they came into camp on a run right into the rope corral. The cook had breakfast going on the stove, red hot. He always cooked a big pot of oatmeal and raisins cereal. Now, it was boiling on the stove and he was busy mixing up a batch of hotcake dough. Bobby ducked her head under the rope and ran right up to the cook tent, shoved her nose into that oatmeal, and was eating it. Cookie looks around and sees her and after her he goes waving that spoon in the air like a club – dough flying in the air and Bobby running away with her nose held high with steam trailing back like a steam engine. I'd like to tell you the conversation coming from Cookie. But, I don't know how to spell those nasty words.

Now, in three or four days, all the skin peeled off Bobby's nose; sure looked funny. You can't write things like this, you can only see them to appreciate it all.

Then, we had this pair of mules that were real camp robbers. They'd get into oats, pellets, or groceries if you were sitting on them, but good pack mules are real honest. When we had a layover day, they seemed to have watches in their heads. At noon, we'd set out a bunch of lunch stuff on the table. Anyone who was hungry made himself a sandwich, or bowl of fruit and coffee or Tang as he or she pleased.

Now, these two long eared Jackasses would come wondering into camp. They'd stand out there, side by side, close to the end of the table, just as close as they dared. Old Jack would always be closest to the cook fly and table. Every little bit, he'd sidestep a little closer. Everyone was watching – big fun. When he got within eight or ten feet of the table, someone would turn a loaf of bread so's the closed end was near the edge of the table, back off, and join everyone watching. Old Jack would sidestep a bit closer and go to step again. Molly would sidestep over next to him and they'd both stand there sound asleep. When Jack figured the time was right, he'd make a big jump at the table, grab that loaf of bread by the butt end and dash for freedom.

As he dashed off, the slices would fall out of the sack along the ground. Molly, with her nose to the ground, would run after him, picking up those slices just like the best vacuum cleaner ever built. Jack would take sack and all. Then, they'd head out to where the other horses were feeding. No one ever chased them away. Everyone enjoyed their act like a real movie at noon.

Chapter Two

How We Got There

Well, along in the late Twenties, me and my brothers really became hooked on hunting, fishing, and trapping. It just seemed to us that plain everyday work was for someone else. We knew it was a waste of time when there was so much to see in those high mountains to the north and east.

Every time we were around a group of the older men, all we heard was hunting and trapping stories. All of them came out of the great South Fork country – now the Bob Marshall Wilderness area. Old Bob Marshall was walking that country at this time.

First, we hunted the Cooper Lake range, not the bottom but the tops. No self-respecting bull or muley buck would hang around the bottoms. Besides, from the top of Mineral Mountain or Daly Peak, you could look into the South Fork and Scapegoat Mountain areas. Many a hunt was dreamed up right there on top of those rocky ridges. They all came to past as our whiskers grew stiffer.

We make our first trips on the fringe of our dreams, taking some friends who wanted to hunt as bad as we did.

One day, a doctor. friend, after a successful hunt says, "Boys, listen to me. You should be charging for this service and make some money." Now, money sounded good to us; we'd never had over $1.00 in our pockets at one time. Our answer was, "You can't charge your friends to go hunting with you." He came back, "If your hunt isn't good enough for your friends to pay for, it isn't good enough for strangers to want."

How right old Walt was. I will remember one trip we had with this attorney who was young, big, and claimed he was tough. We're getting out stock, etc., ready to go the afternoon before and this guy says to Gene he was to be the guide. (Me? I'm the camp tender and cook) "Why don't we just hunt up over Ovando Mountain and drop down to camp in the Dick Creek Basin." Gene says, "That's a long piece and steep. It's a tough trip." He comes back, "You don't think I'm tough enough? Why I can make it and carry you on my back." This is the wrong thing to say. Gene is a little guy, 5'6" and 130 lbs. You never tell a guide you can outwalk him, let alone carry him on your back. Gene says, "Let's go."

"Where will you be camped?" he says to me.

I says, "Wherever I can find wood, water, and horse feed in the Upper Basin."

He says, "Oh, I'll find you, see your smoke or something."

Now I like to rib people who shoot off their mouth so I says to this joker, "Tell you what, you better take off that tie from around your neck cause you'll need lots of air." He's dressed in an uptown suit.

"Don't you worry, he says, I'll need it to drag this kid to camp."

Well, next morning, away we go, me and my pack string, Gene and his 'Charlie Atlas' hunter.

I got camp set up around 3 o'clock and had supper going good. It's getting close to sunset and I hear someone holler my name very faint. I climbed upon a rocky outcropping overlooking the north side of Ovando Mountain and yelled back. Finally, I heard what I thought was someone bringing me a saddle horse over here.

I saddled old Silver, a big guy, and headed down the mountain. It was steep and covered with thick timber. When I reached the creek bed, it was just as steep as a cow's face up the other side. I yelled and Gene says, "Leave the horse and come help me get him over these logs." Now this guy is six feet and 225 pounds, at least. Gene and I racked him over logs, under logs, through a jungle of timber.

But, finally, there in the creek bed is a sight, old Silver. Now we have to load this old boy on a sixteen-hand horse who wants to go to camp. Our friend is about as stiff as a wet dishrag and no power. We get him up there and I lead the horse back to camp. Gene is behind hanging on to Silver's tail for help up the hill. He's worked this old boy as far as he can go.

With Howard at the lead, a packstring on one of his trips stops under the stunning facade of the Chinese Wall in the Bob Marshall Wilderness.

We make the last few steps to camp and unloaded our boy. I put Silver up and came back to camp to finish supper. Now, as I walk in the tent, Mr. Hunter is drinking a Coffee Royal. He looks up at me, jerks off that silly tie, and says, "Here, I won't need this anymore."

We didn't hunt. Next day, we loaded up and took our man home. Seemed like he'd strained some muscles, if he had any, and couldn't walk. His last remark was, "Plenty of game, no spirit."

Right here, on this trip, we both learned a valuable lesson. Don't pay any attention to your guest, just watch his breathing and color and how he travels, and you'll come out okay. So will the guest. It's no fun loading a two-hundred-pound person by rope on a big horse, on a steep sidehill, and in the dark. Worse yet, if he's dead. You have to learn. They'll find out you're tough enough to stay with them.

In the hundreds of people I've guided, I've only seen three men who could make me say 'Uncle' on the mountainside.

Oh yeah, you should have seem some of the pack stock we used and the equipment at first. It would make you cry. We didn't care how rank or what they looked like. If they could pack a load, we used them. Today, I wouldn't give them to my worst enemy. I'd rather shoot him. Now that's all we could afford, so we made them do.

The old adage goes "never look a gift horse in the mouth" and that's what they were – stuff other people couldn't handle. But, I'll tell you what. Them old nags made horse and mule hands out of us two boys. Talk about spoiled bronco nags – we had them, a good foot rope, and an idea of how to use it.

Now things were going a little better with some cash coming in and we got more choices about stock. Also, we'd picked up some bucks and learned the art of throwing the diamond hitch and the double diamond hitch, how to really load an animal and keep her up on top. We were in business. Even got an outfitter license. Now we were legal. Word got around about our ability and game and out-of-state hunters wanted to give us a try. At this stage in life, I still think word of mouth is the best advertisement you can get.

So, away we go, lots of hunting, fishing, and sightseeing parties. We still needed some better pack stock. Coming out of the hills one day, we met two men on the way in. One of them was leading a pair of the prettiest mules you ever saw. After we'd passed them, I hollered at Gene, "We ought to have some of those long ears." He came back, "I'd sure like to have them, too." They looked like two-year-olds. Four or five days later, we met these old boys again. They're headed out, us in. They've got all their stuff packed on two horses and the mules saddles on top. Those two beautiful hard tails are following along behind, happy as if they had good sense. Me, I says to the guy in the lead, "What's the matter with the mule?" He stops and says, "Can't catch those sons of guns. I'm going to sell them as quick as we get home." I says, "What's wrong with right now? How much?" He says, "$75.00 a head." I says, "Ain't no good to me without saddles." He says, "You can have them, too."

Now, he had to go right by our ranch. I says, "When you get to the ranch, turn them in the corral and put the saddles in the shed. I'll be out in a week and send you a check." Didn't think he'd do it but when we got back from that trip, those mules were in the short pasture. That's how I became a mule man.

We used those two Decker pack saddles for patrons and then made us lots more. Fact is, my son is still packing those saddles today, mebby seventy years later. The mules were smart and had the Indian sign on those two old boys. How many years we packed them, I do not recall, but twenty or twenty-five, mebby. They were 1,250 pounds and sixteen hands tall, just right.

Well, along about this time, we're pretty full up with hunters and are camped at the Danaher Ranch. We'd taken a lease from Tom Danaher on his cabins. Really made a nice camp. One big cabin for cook shack and another larger one for bunkhouse.

Old Ben Snoddy came along and wanted us to pack him and his wife in on a hunt. The deal was, we'd put them in a camp close by and they'd do their own hunting and fishing, as they were to stay about all of September. We'd check on them every two or three days and if they got game, Ben would let us know as we left them two old saddle ponies and grain.

Well, this went real fine till one day, in comes Ben and he's lost his wife. He says, "They rode up Calf Creek and tied their horses and took off on foot to hunt. When they got on top a small ridge and stopped for a breather, the Mrs. says, I got a headache, you go on and hunt and I'll just sit around here. Mebby something will come by. I know where the horses are, and I'll wait for you there."

Well, when Ben got to the horses that evening – and no Mary, he hollers and yells, but no answer. He climbs the ridge where he left her and still no Mary. He hollers, yells, and shoots his gun. Still no answer, so he comes for help. We take off to find her. Gene has a gas light. We finally locate the ridge where Ben left her, but can't raise nothing. Gene says, "I'll bet she went down the wrong side so he took off the opposite direction from

A light covering of an early snow blankets the mountains as a packstring heads into the wilderness.

where the horses were tied. Along about 10 o'clock, he hears someone crying. He hollers and yells and finally gets an answer. "I'm here. Can you see my light?"

"Yes", comes back.

He hollers, "Come straight to it, as I come to you." He kept going down this very gentle grassy ridge. She's still down in the creek bottom. He hollers, "Can you see my light?"

"Yes!"

"Well why don't you come so's we can go to camp?"

She hollers, "I'm not lost. I'm going to stay here."

He finally gets to her sitting on a log by the creek crying. She won't move. She wants Ben. He says, "Why didn't you come to meet me?"

She says, "I told Ben I'd wait where he tied the horses and he came and moved them."

"Your horses are clear over the side of this ridge on Calf Creek."

"No, they ain't," says she.

"Ben moved them."

Finally, he's got her back to camp and when he left to come home, she was still giving Ben a going over for moving the horses and trying to get rid of her. Ben ended up with one of the biggest five point bull elk heads I ever saw but Mary, she tended camp from then on.

Now about this time, we hired a camp cook. He was an old time guide, packer, and horseshoer and a pretty fair cook. Now old Virgil was a Kentucky hillbilly who came to Montana many years ago. He was a pretty fair roundup cook and done a good job if you didn't mind a few elk and deer hairs in the soup. Sort of a jolly guy full of strange superstitions. One I always got a bang out of was when he went to bed, he'd always turn his shoes upside down under his cot. Now, he claimed if he didn't, he'd have cramps in his feet and legs all the next day. I always got up and started the fires and got coffee going. Some nights after he went to sleep, I'd turn his shoes upright, then when I got up, I'd turn them upside down. Old Virgil would go through the day happy as a June bug but if he found them upright, he'd be the most miserable cook and hobble around all day cussing his leg cramps.

Now there is no one not even the Boss Man that can keep a happy camp better than a cook. As the old saying goes, "The way to a man's heart is through his stomach." Now, ladies, this also applies to you. The hardest crew member to find is a cook. Lots of people can cook up a storm but that's not good enough. A camp cook has to be a special breed of cat. First off, he can't be afraid of work. He's got to be one jump ahead of everybody in camp. Have a disposition of friendliness mixed with humor and understanding of people who are in a strange element and ask many questions. The cook is supposed to know all answers. Where the game is, what the fish bite and why that saddle makes my butt sore.

It always seems when you find such a cook, he is a good friend of "John Barleycorn" whisky. So the boss man has a problem of how to handle him and keep him happy.

I've had these problems and learned to work around them. I'll tell you about one or two such cases. Now they are just fun to tell about at first it made me sweat getting around them, but we did.

Howard adjusting the packs along the trail.

Number one was a guy called Dutch. He came from Holland as a kid. Very ambitious. When he landed in our country he became a trapper, then a logger, ranch hand and carpenter. Ending up cooking for me. What a great guy and he could know everyone's likes and dislikes by the second meal. It seemed he had a special side dish for some one each meal at the table or in their lunch bag. Every one loved Dutch and his screwy sayings. Like, "them hotcakes are golden black, just like your mother wished she could make them." Or, "Come and get it, Cincinnati chicken and hen, fry it, wash it down with a cup of mud and get the hell out of my kitchen, ain't no elk in here. I got some pearl divin' to do and cook a roast for your supper."

If some one sat down at the table with their hat on, he'd knock it off and say, "Ain't your Daddy taught you no respect." Now amidst the laughter that unlucky lad would grin but not pick up his hat till after the meal was over.

Everyone respected Dutch and offered any help they could give him.

Now they also supplied him with his favorite beverage.

I always cautioned every one not to set a jug in the kitchen and tell Dutch to help himself. Just an evening drink was fine, but no more. Usually this worked out very well. Once in a while some kind hearted guy would not believe me and leave a bottle of jungle juice for him. You could always tell when this had happened. As you neared camp on the way home you could hear Old Dutch singing and smoke coming out of both ends of the cook tent. I'd know the steak was burned and I'd have to finish cooking supper and clean up the kitchen. Next morning at four o'clock you'd hear pots rattling and his soft whistle of some Dutch tune. Then as I stopped for coffee before chores, he'd say, "Things sort of got out of hand last night." I'd answer, "What you mean, I didn't notice anything strange," and all went lovely till the next guest gave it a try. These two times, the guy that was so generous helped me clean up the cook tent and dishes after a hard day's hunt. Now if I had jumped all over him and got mad, he would of put his old sloppy hat on and headed down the trail on foot and I knew that. He was as independent as a hog on ice.

Now you've read this far, mebby you'll finish this tale.

Chapter Three

Before Many Years

Along about now, we booked a nice party from the "Fish, Fin

& Feather Club" in Chicago, all of them dry fly fishermen. We ended up camping on the famous White River where it dumps into the South Fork of the Flathead River, just across from Murphy Flats.

This area along both rivers was known worldwide as some of the best dry fly water for large and beautiful cutthroat trout up to four pounds. We called them flats or red bellies. The water was three degrees colder than ice and streams were so clear you could see the fish's eyes and watch them rise to strike your fly. With spectacular high mountain peaks, with heavy fir timber topped with snow and clear blue skies, it was unbelievable. A camera only messed it up. You have to witness it to appreciate it.

In this party was a lady by the name of Stella. Funny how I can remember her name. It's only been sixty-two years ago that I last saw her, plus she was married at that time. But, could she ever throw a fly line. She'd reach out there two-thirds of the way across the river and set that fly on the water without a swell or ripple. Just like a bee sitting on a rose, and she'd squeal when a big trout would come up and grab it. She had won the champion flycasting contest of the nation a couple of years in a row. Her husband was an excellent man with a fly line, also. It's a pleasure to watch an artist work and she sure was an artist with that piece of bamboo and a string.

She kept asking about that pretty river we rode by on the way into White River, "Is there any fish in there?" That river was the North Fork of the Blackfoot River.

"Yes, it's the best fly stream in the country," Gene tells her, "but due to the big rocks and swift water, it's awful hard fishing."

Now, the North Fork is a swift, rocky stream, clear as a mirror with rapids and big boulders with deep pools around them. Here, the water is 10 degrees colder than ice and hard walking on those slick rocks but great fishing for red bellies and trout and bull trout. He tells her about the North Fork Falls that pours over the edge of the cliffs of the canyon and falls eighty feet into this big blue pool that's full of fish. It really is a spectacular sight of red, white, and copper stained green rocks in the water, and on the banks and walls of the canyon. Foam, white as snow, floating over rapids and green deep pools.

"Why don't we go there?"she asks.

"I 'spose we could on the way home if everybody wants to cut our stay here by a couple of days. Then, we'd go right out to the ranch from there."

Stella isn't long selling her idea to the rest of the party. Well, our camp plans are changed and in a couple of days, we're headed back up river through the Danaher and down the Dry Fork to North Fork Falls.

We camp on the North Fork below the falls and they fish the North Fork below and up the canyon that evening having a real ball. It's much different than the lazy South Fork and just as good fishing.

I forgot to tell you this Stella gal is also hooked on a camera. If she isn't tying on a dry fly, she's stuffing film in a camera. Next morning, Gene, Stella, and her husband and another couple head for the falls. To get up to the falls, you take a trail up a steep mountainside around a high rocky point above the station. Then, you come out of a deep draw onto a open, grassy hillside and look right down over the high red cliffs as the water pours over and down eighty-five feet to a big, blue pool with gobs of snow white foam floating around big boulders and down the river canyon. Up above the sheer cliffs of the canyon, the hillsides are covered with dense Douglas fir and lodgepole pine, a sight no artist could paint.

They tie their saddle horses and go over to the edge, where Stella is working this camera over time. All of a sudden she says to Gene, "Could you guys let me down over the edge to that ledge so's I can take pictures up at the falls as the water comes over."

"I don't know if we can pull you back up," says Gene, "it's thirty-five feet down to that ledge."

"Oh, she don't weigh over one-hundred pounds soaking wet," says

The tranquil setting of one of Howard's camps deep in the heart of the wilderness.

her husband. Now, he's a big guy.

"Oh, I can pull her up myself," says the other guy, who is well fed too.

You should try tying a rope on twenty-five pounds of salt and let it down sixteen feet off a building and try to pull it back up. On the end of that rope, it'll weigh one-hundred pounds. Just you try it!

I wasn't there, but I imagine Gene tied a boatswain chair with his rope forming two loops right together so's she could stick one leg through each loop making a chair or sorts to sit in. Then, you hold onto the rope and are let down in a sitting position. Down over the cliff goes Stella and her camera, no pain or strain. She lands on this ledge on the cliff with lots of room to take her pictures.

"Haul me up, I'm getting wet from the spray," comes her voice over the edge. The boys start pulling on the rope hanging over the cliff. The harder they pulled, the more she became stuck in the ropes on the edge of the rocks. All of the power was going out of the boy's arms. After all, there's only one hundred and ten pounds of female down there. Pretty soon, Stella is yelling, "Pull me up, I'm freezing and my legs are hurting."

Gene says, "Hang on to that rope, if you let go, you'll tip over backwards and fall."

"My hands are frozen," a voice comes back. "Pull!"

The gentlemen on top are counting, "One, two, pull together, one two, pull." Finally, the top of a blonde head sticks up. "Pull again, pull again." Now, some shoulders and a muddy, pale face appears. One of the boys says, "You guys pull and I'll get her by the shoulders." He lays down on the edge of the cliff, gets his arms under hers and a hold of the rope and hollers, "Pull". Up comes Stella and he drags her back away from the edge of the cliff. Resting, she starts to laugh. Now, everyone is laughing except poor Gene. I think he's the only one who realized what a fool trick it was and how close it had been to being serious. If she had lost her cool or panicked, it would have been, "Honey, shut the door, that's all she wrote."

Stella really enjoyed fishing those rough rapids and pools clear down to Smoke's Bridge. Never sent us any pictures if she got any. Only a thank you letter for a wonderful trip. I'll bet no one ever got her into a deal like that again.

One Jump Ahead
(What Makes a Outfitter)

What makes a good outfitter entails a great many things. First, you must love the outdoors and people, also have the ability to learn stock, and your country. How to pick a suitable camp. How to keep your guests out of trouble. In other words, you have to be a half baked psychologist, a veterinarian, know how to put on a band-aid, cook, and shoe horses and be one jump ahead of everyone on the trip. If you're

A quiet pool on a meandering stream in the wild country, the perfect setting for a day of flyfishing.

Preparing for an evening meal of fresh-caught trout.

caught with your pants down, you're in trouble. Also, make time to tell stories. It's all cow college without going to school.

I've tried to explain the horse and mule end of it, but this is just as important. Number one, you should know the country well enough so's you know where you want to camp. When you get there, watch for good grass on any park or hillsides with little timber. Your stock have to eat too. Now, picking a camp you should know where your storms come from. Pick a place near water and timber between you and the wind. Don't forget dry wood close to camp. Try to pick a dry, flat spot. Never camp in a damp, low spot. A flash cloud burst can flood you out in the night quick. Be sure all tentage is anchored solid, the wind can take a tent just like a kite. My motto is, "Grass, Wood and Water." I've seen those who looked for beautiful scenery. A number one in an outfitter's job to become a top outfitter or guide is to learn how to make your guest see all this beauty through your eyes. He is not used to what he's seeing all around him, you have to point it out as you see it. Scenery is wonderful, but no help in a storm and in the mountains, sunny days have a habit of bringing up thunderstorms and without good wood, water and grass, you're in trouble.

In a country like the Bob Marshall Wilderness, most outfitters only bell the leaders and turn loose every thing else, keeping up only wrangled horses. When a bell mare sees you coming, they will usually head for camp on a trot or lope, shaking that bell good and stock out in the brush almost always will take after them as they don't want to be left alone.

Usually the only ones you have trouble with are strays not used to the bunch yet. Some times when you miss some stock, your first bet is to check your back trail for tracks headed out and home.

If I can't hear bells in the morning, I check the back trail first. You will find some areas where horses and mules just don't like and your bell mare will hunt for a place she likes. When she finds it, she'll be there. Remember these spots and check them first. There is one such spot called Meadows Creek, my stock just won't stay there, so we find a narrow spot in the area and sleep there to head them back to camp early in the morning. Just a tip on how to be one jump ahead.

Now with your guest, always try to have some new wrinkle no one else has some thing not expected that no other outfitter does.

I can remember this one well.

I got tired of a dusty floor in the tents as you had to sprinkle with water and sweep clean to make a hard surface each day when camped in the same place for sixty-six days in hunting season. I went to town and found some carpet where a remodeling job was being done. Packed it in and floored my tents. People loved it, so did I. You could slip off your shoes and walk around with warm, clean feet or lay down on the floor. It wasn't long before all the outfitters were covering their floors. Today I do not know a single outfitter who doesn't cover his

Howard with a cup of tea in a photo taken on the "World Council of Tea" incident.

floor with something. More work, but such comfort for your guests after a wet, cold day on the mountain. After you've spent sixty-six days in a tent without floor covering, try the flooring. You'll love it, if you see what I mean – something that no other outfitters give and not advertised in your ad, a welcomed surprise for your guest. It can be like this or something else. But if you are to stay in business, you've got to be one jump ahead.

Tea Council of The World

While word of mouth is by far the best advertisement media there is, here is how it worked with me.

Marg and I spent a lot of money with magazine publishers. One year we took ads in all of the leading outdoor magazines published. We would get as many as twenty-five or more inquires a day and book mebby one of out a hundred. They seemed to be letters from people who just wanted to talk a hunt. Stamps, phone calls, etc., didn't even cover our expenses.

Then one day I got a phone call. It came from the "Tea Council of the World." Whoever they are? They wanted to send a writer and photographer to interview me for a promotion deal to be published world wide. Me, I says "This is for free advertising worldwide and I get paid for it. Just like money from home."

It's late in the fall and the stock is on winter pasture, so I go and get me a couple of mules and saddle horses such as they want. When these gentlemen arrive I'm ready, saddle horses and mules all packed.

Now what they want is a scene of a mountain man kneeling down by an open campfire out in the woods, with a teapot hanging over the fire and me drinking tea and warming my hands by the open fire. Also, the tab of the tea bag must be in plain sight having over the side of the cup so you can read "This Is Tea" on the tab.

The snow is about fourteen inches deep and a cold wind is blowing, not a nice day at all. Well, after much fuss and re-poses, we head for the house to warm up. These boys are not dressed very heavy. Marg has hot soup and coffee and after a warm up, these boys write me a check for fifty dollars with a promise of a set of pictures, and away they go.

Now fifty dollars ain't much, even back then. But it's money!

When we sent the check to the back, we found out it had to cashed on a certain date or it was no good. You guessed it! It was no good. Well, we might get some good from the ads – but not one inquiry, to date, and that's been a lot of years ago. This is a nice picture, don't you think. But I think word of mouth advertisement beats these celebrity shows all to pieces. Even when word of mouth has been stretched like a blown-up balloon.

Chapter Four

How It Was in The 1930's

Now along about this time, we were camped at the old
Danaher Ranch at Danaher. We had lots of game, elk, deer, and
mountain goat, due to light hunting pressure and the start of the
vegetation after big fires and migration from the exploding herds of the
Sun River Game Range. From the time we'd leave the ranch till we
reached camp twenty-nine miles northwest, we'd see lots of elk and
mule deer on both sides of the trail, parked on a mountain, or running
across the trail in front of you.

You know I've spent the bulk of my eighty-seven years right in
this beautiful country in a tent with wild game of all kinds just outside.
Warm, wet or cold, I have never ceased to feel so fortunate just to be
here and enjoy it. Has it changed? Well, so have I, I am grey-headed
and have some gimpy legs but the country and game have been my big
fortune and life.

We'd usually pack the rifles on a mule so's the guests couldn't
shoot on the trail. If they did, we'd have to stop and dress and cut up
the meat, slowing us up in travel time. You see, it was twenty-nine
miles from the ranch to our hunting camp. That meant eight to nine
hours in the saddle for our guests as they could not travel as fast as the
pack strings. Had to have rest periods and a break for lunch. Us old
hands ate as we rode and stopped only when it was necessary to adjust

a pack.

I've had elk run into my pack string four times in one day, causing a wreck. Most generally, it was some calf who was behind a bunch that had already crossed in front of me. He'd probably been left sleeping, woke up and says, "I got to catch up with ma."

On this trip I just spoke of, I'd had to stop and tie my string back together three times already. I only had a mile and a half to go. I got it made, thinks me. I'm traveling along a hillside trail with the creek down below. When out of the brush comes this calf, right up to my passing mules! He's spooked and looking them over. I sped up my saddle horse hoping to get the last three mules by. But no luck. He sees daylight between two of them mules and says, "I can jump over that lead rope." He jumps, the mule sees him and hauls back raising that lead rope about one foot, tripping that elk in mid-air and rolling him down the hill into the creek. Surely goosed those old long ears but they

The stunning panorama of the interior of the Bob Marshall Wilderness. This is the wild country that was the setting of Howard's activities for many years.

led faster the rest of the way to camp. I don't think that calf ever tried that again as he sure left a spray of water and loose elk hair in the air.

Now, along about this time, we booked two doctors on a hunt. It was a one on one deal as they were strictly trophy hunters who wanted nothing but big-horned bulls. Both were middle aged, husky boys but carrying too much weight – not real mountain men. After three or four days on the hill, it was sort of slowing up their power and speed. I suggested an easy day to Doc Bryant. "Let's take an easy one today. I need a rest." This sure pleased the old boy, I could tell.

Well, we left camp on foot that morning cause he was a bit tender where the saddle fit and I planned on easy country close to camp. It was a beautiful area, gentle slopes, big, heavy timber, and no downfall or brush. There were some rocky ravines where small creeks flowed down to the valley floor. Real pretty country with small open hillsides and open parks. Used heavily after snowfall, but a main crossing for

Pack string on the move.

Loading up.

bulls in the rut when looking for a girl friend.

In this type of area, you can gain a lot of altitude without too much effort and your hunter won't realize he's climbing, sort of a con game between hunter and guide with the hunter not knowing it. Well, along about 10 o'clock, I picked up a bugle and figured I had a lover looking for love. I climbed up and around where he was. Got the wind in my favor and slipped in close and hid by a big old juniper to stay out of sight. Gave him a couple of calls and he'd answer me right back each time but would not move. We kept this yodeling at each other till about noon and he shut up. Wouldn't answer at all

I said, "He's bedded and is going to stay put till later this afternoon. We might just as well take it easy here in the shade till about 4 o'clock and he'll start to move and we'll get a look at him."

Well, Doc lays back, puts his hat over his eyes, and starts to snort right sudden.

There is a ravine right between us and this bull, only we're about a hundred yards up above where he's bedded. I slip over on my belly and take a peek to see how the land looks below. Now, if that bull tries to cross the ravine, he'll roll rocks and expose himself on an open parky hillside that we can see by standing up. A perfect place to catch him. I crawl back to the juniper and wait. Sure like to snooze in this sunshine like Doc, but I got to listen if Mr. Bull Elk decides to move out.

Along about 3 o'clock, I hear some rocks roll, not loud, but rocks don't roll by themselves so's I ease over and peek around a boulder and sneaking up this ravine, right to us, slowly comes a big six-point bull. He's wondering where that other noisy bull went to and is about to find out.

I gently wake Doc and whisper what's cooking to him. He grabs his rifle and I ease him over to the edge of the ravine so's he can see the bull. He eases up his rifle and down falls the elk. Before I can say or do anything, Doc is over the edge and running to his elk. I yelled, "Stop!" But, he can't hear anything now. He grabs that bull by the antler and does that bull come alive. With one shake of his head, Doc flies through the air down the ravine. The bull spins right after him dragging his hind legs. I jump after them pulling my handgun. I beat Doc to the bull and shoot the bull in the head. The elk, now dead, rolls down on top of Doc. When I have Doc out of that bloody mess, he's yelling "Ain't he a dandy!"

Now, I'm thinking something else. I don't know if Doc ever realized how close he came to that being his last hunt.

Howard and Margaret Copenhaver in Seattle, Washington, in 1944.

Chapter Five

The Navy Years

In 1941, this old boy over across the Atlantic called Hitler was causing a lot of trouble and someone waved a flag under my nose. I'm a patriotic son who believes in fairness and freedom of speech. I figure it's my duty to do my part. After all, I'm tough and a good shot so away I go to Missoula. I looked my choices over and decided the Navy needed me. I didn't like the sound of digging holes in the muddy ground, then trying to hide in them while somebody's shooting at me.

At least in the Navy, I'd have my groceries close by, a roof over my head, and if the ship sank, I could swim. They told me salt water was easy to swim in. I didn't realize how much salt water there was out there. Or, that they had so many beans stored in that galley. You'd think those cooks would get tired of cooking beans every day, day after day, but they never ran out. Also, had plenty of red lead and mud called coffee.

I never got too much of an education, as in high school, I majored in girls. They did keep me an extra half a year. It seems algebra and I didn't get along and without it, I couldn't get that piece of paper with a ribbon tied around it, the one my folks thought I needed. I figured they needed me as a good example for those freshmen coming along.

I got a real education in the Navy. I always figured the greatest bit of knowledge and best a man could get – not book learning but just what makes people and the world turn around. I found out right quick. Whatever I was the best at, there was always a guy just a bit better that I had to figure a way around him.

Right here I should tell you of my first work detail in Uncle's Navy. We were at quarters the first morning. This Cranky Snappy Old Chief called us to order and read from a piece of paper.

"Copenhaver. step out," he said, snappy and sharp. Along with four others, I stepped out. "You sailors report to the Spud Locker." We finally found it was where they stored one-hundred-pound sacks of potatoes. A cook standing there says, "You guys pack all the spuds out side and clean this locker then stack them back and report to me."

This locker is connected to the galley – or kitchen. We bailed right to and would lift up a sack, throw it over a shoulder, turn and walk out the back door of the galley and pile it. The dust was piled about four inches deep on the last few sacks (Saturday morning); made no difference to us. I stepped in and threw this dirty sack over my shoulder. Ker-bump! I hit something, I turned around and there stands Captain Needles and his inspection crew all in whites (except the Captain, he sure was covered with spud dust). I dropped the sack, he saluted me and says, "Carry on sailor, I have no business being in your way."

My first encounter with brass, but I had an idea he wasn't just another sailor.

Anyway, I came home with campaign bars, Pacific and Asian ribbons, Purple Heart, and seven little gold stars representing major engagements and sea battles and a "hitch in my get along." I do not regret a day of it all. It was my way through cow college and that guy upstairs sure looked over me, while many were not so fortunate.

Now, I'm back where I belong in the mountains of old Montana with my mules.

You know I could tell you so many war stories and horrible

ones. But they're hard to talk about and are all summed up in one phrase, "War is Hell!" I'll tell you now of the greatest sight a man could ever see and may it never happen again.

We got orders to leave the front lines and steam to the Marshall Islands. When we got there, the sea was covered with ships, troop ships, tankers, ammunition ships, chow wagons, destroyers, cruisers, gun boats, aircraft carriers, and battle wagons – some fresh out of dry dock, others newly commissioned. Our crow's nest was 109 feet above the water line. We headed out that day to who knows where. I could look with binoculars as far as I could to the east, south, and north. I saw nothing but solid lines of ships headed west. No one said but we all knew Leyte Gulf and Philippines, here we come. And, we did.

What a great sight, when you've been out there so long with a fleet so small that the Japanese had us out-powered ten to one. You were proud to belong to a country that could do this in such a short period of time; not just me, but every sailor on board the old Maryland BB46. You all know how it ended, so's I'll leave it right here.

Back home in 1946, with one month to set in hunting camps, get guides, and stock ready for elk season. My season was pretty full and Gene and Wendel were still working for Uncle Sam. Gene was still in Germany and Wendel was in the Air Force some place.

I rounded up some boys to help me. They didn't know the country or the finer points of guiding but we did it anyhow. My first party was eight men from Michigan. It turned out to be the most miserable hunting trip I ever experienced. When I got out and settled up with them, I asked them never to contact me again. There were three or four of them that were gentlemen and good men, but the others were bums. The leader of the bunch was a draft dodger who bought cars for nothing from kids drafted and sold them after the war for three times their worth to the same kid he bought them from in the first place.

He'd get up long before daylight to put on a pair of track shoes and head out. He'd shoot a bull, come back to camp and say to one of the party, "This is your bull," and take off again. He wouldn't go with me to show me where the elk laid. I had to hunt it up myself. It's hard to hunt a live bull but try finding a dead one in rough timbered country. After he'd done this three times, I took his gun and threatened him with citizen arrest. In other words, I grounded him. His hunting partners were mad and backed me up. From then on, it was an awful nasty camp. Sure was no way to start a season.

In all my years of outfitting, it never happened again. I can only praise my guests over the years as gentlemen and sportsmen. As a whole, they were some of the greatest men and women I've ever met. The pleasure has been mine.

Howard and Margaret Copenhaver in the 1950's.

Chapter Six

Cooper Lake Fishing

Y a know, I've always been a hunter but that don't mean I'm not a fisherman, too. I love to fish. It's just like hunting. I can fish all day and never get a fish. Just being out there with nature; sitting and enjoying the beauty of the stream, lake, or mountains. The poem someone wrote, *"Only God Can Make a Tree"* surely proves who made the rest of these great mountains, lakes, and streams. The network of how they all fit together is mind boggling to us who love them so much. Just to sit and think, listen to the wind, and the voices of the wilds. It makes a man feel so small and humble. But, it's good for you. I couldn't enjoy life without it. Sort of recharges your batteries.

Cooper's Lake is such a place. In summer, it's beautiful and in winter, six feet of snow and ice, it's another thing – but beautiful. The mountains rise straight up to 7,000 and 8,000 feet, covered with heavy timber to timber line, then craggy cliffs sticking out of the white, white snow, capped by the blue sky. You can't beat it. With a fishpole in your hand, a cup of coffee in the other, and a bonfire to warm your bones, I love to fish, especially since the years have crawled up on me. No hills to climb. No downfall to fight or cutting a trail to get those mules up to your game. Just pull them out of the hole in the ice and go for another one.

What a life with great friends who are just as hooked as you are.

Right here, I'm going back one long piece. I'm ten or eleven years old. Some neighbor boys and my brother get a promise out of our dads we'll all go fishing and camp all night up at Cooper's Lake and fish for two days.

We'd drive up to old lady Lawrence's place and leave the team and sleigh there, then walk up the creek to the lake. Everyone had a pack on his back. It was only three-quarters of a mile hike to the lake. Nothing to it. We'd done it many times in the summer catching red bellies out of the creek as went.

Now, I must tell you about the fish in this lake. They were different than most trout because when they spawned, they'd go downstream; other fish go upstream in small, gravelly streams. Cooper Lake had no good spawning holes upstream.

Today, we have Yellowstone cutthroat and west coast cutthroat. These back then were black-spotted, native cutthroat that everyone called "red bellies." They had a bright red cutthroat with a flaming red belly, even the pan fry were bright colored with dark backs. Very beautiful fish with bright pink meat.

In the spring, they'd come down from Rock Creek from the lake filling the creek solid where the gravel bars were. People would come up there in their old Model T's, Chevy's, and Packards when the run came on to fish. They'd walk along the creek with a pitchfork and throw the fish out on the bank. Or, have a gunny sack with a hoop in the open end, dig a ditch in the gravel bar where it hit the riffles, place the open end of the sack upstream, then run the fish downstream. When they'd come to the riffles, they'd run in and lift up the open end of the sack. Then, drag it back to the bank and dump the fish on the bank, sometimes going home with a sack of trout. When they got home, they'd can them for summer's meat. Now I know this was wrong, but it's the way some people did. As years went by, it killed the fishing in the lake. Much like the salmon in the Columbia and streams in Alaska.

Well, on with my story. Bill Lawrence decided to go with us. He comes out with a toboggan about ten feet long and says tie your stuff on this, then you can take turns pulling it. Also he's got a couple of pair of extra snowshoes. Now, Ezra has a pair so Dad and Ernie Tubbs put on the extra pairs and are going to pack a trail for us kids to pull this toboggan with all our camp gear, etc. loaded on it. These old boys are not dumb. They take their fishing gear with them. Now there are five of us kids. We should have no trouble with that toboggan and gear. Their snowshoe trail held us up good till we got in the narrow canyon where the sun never hit and the snow did not have a crust on it.

The packed trail would hold us fine until we pulled on that toboggan. Then, we'd go through the snow up to our waist or more. I'll tell you, it was an uphill battle till we hit the steep narrow side hill, the last half mile. We'd sink up to our necks and the toboggan would slide downhill to the brush along the creek. We'd have to unload, get our sleigh back on the trail, then load all the gear, and away we'd go again for 100 feet. Then load it again. Don't get discouraged, there's fish up ahead. Let's go. Finally, we can see the log jam at the end of the lake. We got her whipped.

At last we're on flat ice and the lake. Now, way off, up the lake are three guys having a big time, catching our supper. I for one was so tired I couldn't walk out that far on the ice, plus they'd built a fire along the bank so that's where we parked the toboggan and five mountain men in the making or ending. Didn't care much which, at the time.

Now if you think book learning is hard to get, try this sometime. It 'pears to me, over the years, book knowledge don't last like the real thing, with plenty of sweat and hurt. The hurting leaves, but the smell of sweat don't and it all ends up into enjoyment in later years.

Well, after about an hour, Gene digs out the fishing gear and him and Perry head out across the lake. Then goes Lawrence. Frank and I just don't have that much ambition. After awhile, we can see them boys are catching fish, so away we go. Sort of slow and easy. When we got out there, don't think we've even got a bite yet, when along comes the old man and hollers, "Come on you guys, we're going to set up camp and get supper." Sun's getting close to the tops of those mountains and it's chilling off. So away we go. Me, I can stand some groceries anyway.

We get a big bonfire going and set up a lean-to with a tarp and some poles with the fire out in front. Our beds were under this fly. The fire reflects into the lean to tent on the open side. Right comfortable, but a little hot on the front side. You got to keep turning to feel good.

Supper is half-baked fish, burnt on one side and raw on the inside. I end up like dad, broiling a ham steak on a willow over the coals. Hot coffee and a slice of bread really brought the soul and body together again. Then somebody turned out the light and we had only campfire to see by.

When they started the fire, they did not make a base for it. Just padded the snow down hard with their snow shoes. We turned in for a night's rest with the instructions, if we woke up, we were to put wood on the fire. You know who was going to wake up? Us kids! As we kept the fire going, the heat reflected off the lean-to tent and melted the snow and the fire sank lower into the snow and so did the snow at the foot of us kid's beds. So, pretty soon we were sliding down into the pit about four feet deep around the fire. Finally, we're up and sitting on the snowbank around the fire. What a night of rest. Between the smoke in that hole and the heat from the fire, you'd burn on one side and freeze on the other.

Well, breakfast is over and the sun's coming up and we're going fishing. Bill Lawrence says to Gene and me, "I'm going across the lake to those rock cliffs. There's really a good hole over there. If I wave, you come running."

We're getting a fish once in a while, but it's pretty slow. Then, we see Bill waving. Away we go. Now he has three holes all close together, cut through the ice and several fish on the ice. As we walk up, Bill is just pulling a trout out of the lake. He says to Gene, "Quick drop your hook down there." Gene drops his hook in that hole and bingo, out he comes with a nice one. Bill yells at me, "Drop your hook in there, quick!" I did, and bang, I had one. Out he comes and Bill drops his hook in and out comes another one.

We kept this up for quite a while as I remember when the school of fish moved off, we'd caught somewhere in the thirties in number. All of these fish were old red bellies from twelve to eighteen inches long, the most beautiful trout you ever saw.

Then Bill told us, "When you catch a fish, have another pole with a hook on it all ready to drop right back down in because these cutthroat travel in big schools in the winter. When one is hooked and fighting, he attracts the others and they'll hit a black fish hook without any bait. If you keep them excited, they'll stay right around that hole looking for something to eat. If you don't give them something, they'll move on agin." How true he was. I've never seen another lake like that in my life.

Then, we get some bugologist in the game department in the early Thirties and they decide Cooper's Lake should have rainbow trout planted in it. This guy's name was Stubbelfield. They planted lots of rainbow. Now it only took a few short years and the rainbow crossed with the cutthroat and the offspring were sterile and no more trout fish. It became squaw fish and suckers. Still is poor fishing today.

Now, I believe biologists do good and we need them but crossing rainbow and cutthroat does not work. It killed Cooper's Lake and also the North Fork River. The river is coming back to cutthroat trout now and is good, but for many years, it was dead.

Well, this fishing trip was tough, but great, and I'll always remember the good fishing and the effort in ups and downs getting it done.

Since then, I've learned how to build a fire on top of the snow and keep it there and set up a winter camp to be comfortable. Also, how to cook fish done on all sides without burning them on an open fire. There is also this deal of setting up camp first before dark. Fish when the sun comes up. Oh, yes, we gave the fish to old lady Lawrence and all the neighbors on the way home. Also, mom had some real chow for supper that night, even cake and fruit.

There was no smoke or wet blankets that night. Next morning, everyone had forgotten the trials, just remembering the fun of being there and the beautiful fish.

Ice Fishing

There is one disease you can pick up here in Montana and it's wild and free. Once you've contracted it the only cure I know of is more birthdays or just plain lay down and die. Now who wants to die anyway? Yeah, there's still some big fish under that ice. They call it a sport. Ice Fishing's the name.

You get up before day light, hop in the pickup and are gone. Always have plenty of hot coffee and a sandwich cause you never know, might be late tonight. When you get there, there is already nine or ten more silly souls humped up over a hole in the ice looking for the sun or cussing the cold winter wind, wrapped up in so many layers of clothes they look like a pile of rags out there on the ice, slapping their hands and walking back and forth, trying to keep warm. Laughter drifts across the ice and you wonder who told a joke.

When you get out there, greet a few friends and get that hole bored or chopped through the ice and your pole all set, baited and down below.

There's a nice little red and white bobber floating on top the water waiting for a fish to grab that bait and jerk the bobber under the water.

Now you've joined the boys in their warm up dance and cussing the wind.

How do you know there's a fish down below? Well, they sure were here yesterday and some big ones, too. Now get ready for the story of "You should have been here Tuesday. Boys were they biting, I caught several in the third to fifth class. Threw back my limit of small ones the first half hour." They'll start at seven o'clock in the morning.

It's ten thirty in the morning now and I'm watching that bobber keeping the ice from freezing it solid. Sitting on a buck trying to set in the middle of my underwear where I can feel some heat. At least a little warmth. Eyes glued to that red and white bobber. It won't move, must be froze down.

Me, I get to thinking. Why in the hell am I here? I could be home with a gas furnace and griping at the children. Mother wouldn't have to listen to all these cockeyed lies and stories. Who can enjoy a good story where he's shivering and has to keep his mouth closed or he'll loose his false teeth. It moved just a bit. I jump and grab that pole and wait. Nothing. Start to set the pole in the holder again. Start to tell the boys I had a nibble when down goes the bobber. Clear below the ice. I grab that pole and give her a jerk. By God! I got one. Boy is that fish in a hurry to get out of there. He gives me a nice battle and I've got him up to the ice. I get a look at him every once in a while.

My buddies are grouped around me. Old Ted says, "Need a gaff hook?" Don't know. He's sure a keeper. Better see if you can gaff him, I've only got six-pound test line. Ted slips that gaff down the hole and waits. "Don't rush him," he cautions. He's huge. I give him some slack and play him some more.

Advice from Wendel and friends: "Give him lots of time. Don't rush him, he'll slow up." Then Ted and I got him and out of that little eight-inch hole Ted hauls a ten-pound rainbow trout. Beautiful with bright red gills, black spot on sides and that red rainbow from gills to tail.

Every body is patting my back sort of warming me up inside and out.

I bait my hook and drop her down that hole again looking at that little red and white bobber. Then I notice the wind has come up and the snow is drifting. Not only that it's snowing and my feet are frozen. Where was all that warm furnace I was dreaming about before that cockeyed fish hit? You talk about a bad cold. This Ice Fishing disease is the worst of all.

Now my friend, Ted Davis, is a great hunter and fisherman, but fly fishing is the summer months. I tell him, "You've got to go over to Brown's Lake fishing with me some time." Well he agrees to go, saying, "I ice fished a couple of times threw the ice when I was a kid and didn't like it." I says, "You didn't know what you were doing."

Anyway, we hit the lake one day and he really had good luck. Limited out and was throwing them back before I caught my limit. You talk about getting hooked on ice fishing, he sure did. When ice times comes now if you see his pick up in the back end is a Polaris 4x4 and fishing gear. He and my brother, Wendel, and I have a running battle to see who gets the biggest. Ted and I both held Wendel down all winter of '99, but Wendel shows up the other day with dandy close to eleven pounds and beautiful so look at next winter, we've got our chores laid out for us.

It don't make any difference what kind of weather, he and Ted are gone to the lake.

One day Ted shows up here and he's got a catalog from a sporting store. In it is a "Fish House Kit" for sale. You buy the kit and build it yourself. It folds up like a suitcase and opens out into a five foot by six foot square house, six and one half feet tall. I says, "I can't stand that cold any more, I'll buy it and you help me build it." Well, we got it all built and I happened into Bob Ward & Sons in Missoula, Montana, and bought a heater. Uses a five-pound propane tank and puts out 29,000 BTU's. Now I can set in there on a chair warm as toast and fish. Made a sled and we pull it out on the lake with a 4x4 or snow machine. Sort of got the Up Town cure on this ice fishing disease.

Surely is nice to set in there in your shirt sleeves drinking coffee, looking out the window at the beautiful mountain peaks and those other guys hunched up froze over a hole in the ice.

The Montana Centennial Train at the New York World's Fair in 1964.

Chapter Seven

How It Happened

There are probably stories of how and why the Montana Centennial Train got started. I'm going to explain it as Howard Kelsey told it to me. He's the guy that started it all in the first place.

Howard owned and ran the Nine Quarter Circle Ranch, a dude ranch up the Taylor's Fork of the Gallatin River, southwest of Bozeman bordering Yellowstone Park. On the west rose the great Spanish Peaks. This is one of the great game areas of southwest Montana containing fish, elk, deer, mountain goats, mountain sheep, grizzly bear and black bear; a sportsman's paradise since Montana was Montana Territory. That's one long piece of time. Beauty, that has not changed.

I was shoeing Howard's stock at the time that he told me this story. They'd had a great day fishing and after supper, were sitting around a campfire talking and viewing the spectacular scenery in the early evening as the stars came out and sunset faded away. The snow-capped, rocky peaks reflected in the mirrored lake and the beauty of the scene was shared by everyone.

One man said, "Howard, Montana should load this all on a train and take it to all the people in the big cities from Frisco to New York and back again. Give them a chance to see it as it is." I had just retired as President of the Outfitters & Dude Ranchers organization the year before. Howard says, "Cope, will the outfitters back this show?" After he told me what his ideas were, I said, "Yes! And, I'll put down the first check when you holler." Howard was a very brilliant man and he meant for you to go ahead and get it done. He was forceful and had a mind like a computer. I knew he'd do it.

He took his plan to the newly formed Centennial Commission and he was voted Chairman of the Centennial Train Committee. He suddenly had Jack Hume as Assistant Director.

Editor's Note: The following excerpt is from a publication about the Montana Centennial Train written by L. W. Upshaw, chairman of the Montana Centennial Commission.

An Idea That Grew to Fantastic Proportions...

It was on a fishing trip at one of the thousands of inspirational spots in Montana than an enthusiastic outdoorsman spoke up and said to his fellow anglers, "We should tell the world more about Montana. Let's fill a train with boosters and tour the country."

The idea was presented to the Montana Territorial Centennial Commission by Howard Kelsey, owner of the Nine Quarter Circle Ranch, and he was promptly named chairman of the Centennial Train Committee. The concept as viewed at first was quite modest but under Kelsey's leadership things began to happen. First, he gained a valuable assistant, Jack Hume.

Kelsey noted that the trains journey east coincided with the opening of the New York World's Fair. After some inquiries, he garnered permission to park the train at the Fair for a three day stay. The train idea fascinated General William F. Potter, Executive Vice President of the Fair, who suggested the Train stay for the two years the Fair is to run. Robert Moses, President of the Fair, concurred and Kelsey set about to make this a reality. Fair officials made available a site with a 350 foot frontage to which was later added an additional 240 feet or the equivalent of two city blocks.

The Train grew from 10 to 25 cars. More cities were added to the itinerary. There was money to raise, problems to solve and regulations to comply with and they had to buy a train. The latter was purchased from the state of West Virginia who had equipped their Centennial Train for travel throughout that State during its Centennial year. From West Virginia Kelsey borrowed Bill Bolden, the Centennial Trainmaster there, to oversee re-fitting of the Train.

To decorate the Train exterior, two fine artists were acquired, Lyman Rice and Bud Wert. The interiors were given to Bob Morgan of the Montana Historical Society to prepare displays. Material for the displays was loaned through Mike Kennedy, Director of the Montana Historical Society. Ott Tschache was added to the staff to manage the

Howard Kelsey (left), who is credited with developing the idea of the Montana Centennial Train, astride his saddle horse in Omaha, Nebraska. In the center background is Bonnie Jo Hunt, Miss Montana Centennial.

Montana exhibit during its stay at the Fair and Bill Briscoe joined the group as an Administrative Assistant. These men were seized with the infectious fervor of Kelsey and Hume and the details and loose ends began to fall into place.

Cooperation was received by many State and Federal agencies as well as privately owned enterprises, all of whom realized the potential to their own organizations. Individuals, far too many to mention even fleetingly here, pitched in to bring the enterprise to fruition. The result is a collection of significant Montana displays championed by Montanans eager to tell about them in the hope that they will attract visitors to the Treasure State. Nor does this dream end in New York. Kelsey is examining an invitation to send a portion of the Train to Europe.

I hope that you can visit the train and meet with Howard Kelsey and Jack Hume and the 300 other friendly Montanans who are actors in this drama.

Chapter Eight

Patches The Queen

Way back in 1962, a group of dude ranchers and outfitters were talking about advertising. Suddenly, Howard Kelsey of the Nine Quarter Circle Ranch out of Gallatin Gateway, Montana, got the floor. He said, "What we ought to do is go East with a train load of horses and pack mules and parade some of those big cities." Everybody laughed and talked about it but no one realized what would come of such a suggestion.

Now, my friend, Howard Kelsey, was not a guy who warmed a chair after getting an idea that sounded good. He got around a campfire up on the Taylor Fork one night with a group of influential men from New York, from Great Falls and Bozeman, Montana, and a plan was born and did it grow! Meeting after meeting, committees, board meetings, on and on. Finally, the Montana Centennial Commission was formed.

Then came the work of raising funds, signing up people to go. And buying a long train and clearing it with railroad companies to use their engines and tracks, plus arrangements with city governments to parade on their streets, advertisements with newspapers, radio stations and television people, and for hotels and banquet space. It goes on forever, but we were expected and very successful. We ended up with parlor cars for the horses and mules, exhibit cars, Pullman cars and dining cars — all owned by the Centennial Commission. Then came the volunteers to help get it ready and work on the trip a total of over 300 people from their teens to the oldest man in Montana, Native Indian dancers and 175 head of horses and mules. There was also plenty of Old Yellowstone whisky, though I never saw a drunk person on the 30-day trip through fourteen of the major cities east of the Mississippi River.

We had exhibition cars with the art from many of the great Montana artists and $1,000,000 in Montana gold, silver and other native gems on display — all because of an old cowboy's dream he wasn't afraid to tell people about.

At the first meeting, I opened my big mouth and said, "Get it off the ground and I'll put up the first check." Well, as you guessed by now, me and Marg were right in the middle of it with two saddle horses and four mules packing kitchen, duffel and meat and antlers up and down the streets. And this is where Patches, my pinto mule, came in. But first, a few things happened along the rail, not the trail I was used to riding.

Now, we had to train all this stock to get used to cars, people, and plenty of noises. They'd never heard a train whistle in the hills of old Montana. Five other guys and I ended up with forty-six head of mules and horses at the fairgrounds in Missoula, Montana. The people of Missoula

Patches The Queen at work in the high country of Montana.

helped us a lot, honking their horns, revving their motors and yelling at us to get out of their way. The police were very cooperative, too. They allowed us to train on the race track and rodeo arena or we couldn't have got it done.

After we got some working pretty good, we'd go out on the streets right down Main Street. Sometimes it was fine, other times the public didn't act as if they enjoyed our show.

One day, Herb Toelke said, "I'm going to hitch all six up today. I think my lead team is shaped up good enough for the streets."

Now, he was driving six head of 16-hand, 1,500-pound colts pulling a big Tallyho Stage. This team is well-matched sorrels with lots of spirit. We got all lined out, made a turn around the race track and headed down the main street for town traffic. All went well till we hit the Higgins Avenue bridge. Right in the middle of the bridge, Herb met a bicycle ridden by a guy whose big, flappy coat was waving in the breeze. These old ponies hadn't ever seen a bicycle before, let alone a live one waving a coat right under their noses. Before you could say "Jack Robinson," those ponies jackknifed and Herb lost the show! Well, the team, Tallyho and Herb were crossways on the bridge, with car horns honking, people screaming advice and a few unprintable sayings at him.

We finally got the nags straightened out, into motion and finished our tour without any further incident.

Just one more. We were in Baltimore, Maryland, parading down the street with hundreds of people on each side enjoying the show when another incident occurred. I was leading my pack mules, all loaded and doing nice, when just like a flash, the pack on my third mule back in the string turned under his belly. Luckily, Marg was able to hold my saddle horse and head mule while I repacked my mule as the rest of the parade went around us. I had lots of volunteer help those on the sidewalk, but was it embarrassing at the time — a hotshot in cold water.

But, back on line with my story in regard to getting ready for the big trip. We had to get all that stock used to parading and also legged up so they wouldn't get stiff walking on all the cement streets ahead of them. Also, they had their long Montana winter hair on them and we had to blanket them to get them to shed it off so they would look nice and slick and clean.

Now, don't you know Old Man Winter changed his mind and turned the temperature down to 28 to 30 degrees below zero. Those horses needed, and grew, hair. We then had but one choice, to clip the hair off with hair clippers. We'd throw a horse, someone would sit on its head, and we'd tie all four feet and go to work. In about four days the job was done. We sure had a pile of horse hair and some mighty sore spots where we didn't move fast enough to miss a iron-shod hoof aimed with mulish accuracy.

Next came the vet deal. Each animal had to have a series of shots for who knows what kind of diseases. Well, we contracted a vet to do all of this and clear the papers for each state we would visit on the tour. This old doc knew his business but old Patches, after the first shot, hated that guy. I could take the needle, go into her stall and give her a shot and all she'd do was jump a little, but if the vet showed up she'd kick that stall to pieces. It got so that the day he was to give another shot, I'd tie her to a hitchrack outside before he came. She got so she knew the sound of his truck and would start to raise Cain before he got close to her.

One day I didn't tie her up in time. The vet showed up and Patches was loose in the box stall with her blanket still strapped on her. She heard his car stop out front and she started kicking the walls and door of the stall. Off flew the door and out came Patches, headed anyplace away from there.

Well, Freddie Deschamps has just gotten his four-horse team hooked up to the hay wagon and he was climbing on to give them a workout on the track when round the barn came Patches on a run, tail and head high and that blanket flapping in the air. Away went Freddie's four-horse team. He made a grab for his lines, got only one, and hauled back, hollering, "Whoa!" They kept going, but he turned them into the race track gate and from then on it was a race — with no holds barred. Those four old ponies decided to leave the country, and right behind came Patches and her blanket. Poor old Freddie; they lost him at the gate. Some thoughtful guy drove a truck across the gate and the race was on.

First they lost the rack and hind wheels, then a front wheel that couldn't dodge a post. By then, the team's spirit was ebbing and the sweat running and the horses kegged up in the far corner of the track, Patches had lost her blanket, and the dust finally settled. We gathered up the pieces and it was decided that what Freddie really needed was a new wagon, a few bandaids, and a good stiff drink to bring heart and mind back together again.

Finally, we got them all in shape and loaded on the train and headed for Billings, Montana, to pair up with the rest of the crew from the east side of the state.

When we unloaded at Billings, everybody wanted to know how we had gotten our stock to shed off and look so nice and slick. So there we went again — clipping horses and trimming tails. Didn't have enough time to finish before we left, so we completed the job in Omaha, Nebraska, before the first parade.

Oh yeah, there was an older bachelor from up by Red Lodge who had brought his Palomino saddle horse, long haired and dirty, right out of the hills. I don't think that horse had ever had a curry comb or brush run over his hide. He looked terrible, but the guy wouldn't let us clip him. Said he was fine. We tried to get him to use a curry and brush because his horse was dirty, but he said, "Never owned a comb! No use for one." One evening we sheared this nag. Well, the next morning this old boy threw his saddle on him, jerked up the cinch, stepped back and looked at his horse. In a loud, booming voice he shouts to the world, "Now that's the way a horse oughta look. Haven't you guys ever heard of a curry comb and brush?"

One of the outrider's with the Indian wagon (named Fred) had a beautiful Appaloosa saddle horse. He had a perfectly spotted blanket of black and white spots over his hips. Now Fred's wife, a redhead with fire enough for two women, was riding an old white horse. Everyone else had matched horses of the same color. We had working with us three young cowboys with more spirit than good sense, Howie, Walt and Gary, who figured this didn't make the rest of our outfit look so good. So, one night they got some India ink and made an Appy out of the white horse. But they didn't stop at that — they drew tepees and Indian sign language all over old Whitey. When Fred and wife came to saddle up for the parade next morning, you should have heard Fred. Was he wild! But due to the compliments they received after the parade, his lovely lady sort of liked it. Fred's complaints wouldn't have made any difference anyway, because you couldn't brush or wash off those signs; any change now had to wait for new hair to grow in. And, until he reads this, Fred has never known who performed this miracle.

After the show in Omaha, we went to Cincinnati, Ohio. Now, the Indian dances were a high spot in the whole show and people were constantly after the dancers to perform on television programs and in night spots. Also, every city we hit was invited to bring the grade school kids to tour the Centennial Train exhibition cars free of charge. So here would come a big line of kids, with a teacher on each end to kind of keep them together, one line after another, all day long, going through the display cars.

One day we were parked at the Central Station in Cincinnati, a huge place. People had to come through a big lobby, going and coming from the cars, and it was a busy place because trains were in use back then.

On this one particular day, the Indian dancers had put on a show somewhere uptown and they were dressed in all the Indian finery, tomahawks and all, and could they dance! Kenny Left Hand was a big, young man and full of the devil. Just as Kenny came into the lobby from the street in all his Indian finery, the school kids were headed out and Kenny let out a warhoop or two and took after these kids, waving his tomahawk, dancing, with all the little bells on his wrists and ankles ringing. You should have seen those kids go.

There was no place to hide, but there was a string of ladies and men toilets along the far wall and the doors flew open and the screaming kids dashed in. Out, just as fast, came women shaking down their dresses and men zipping up their pants. What a riot.

One little boy fell right in the middle of the station. Kenny danced up to him with his tomahawk raised in the air. This kid jumped to his knees, put his hands under his chin, sort of prayer-like, and screamed, "Please no, Mr. Indian." Kenny gently picked him up and gave him some feathers and an Indian headband, and the show was all over. I'll bet that kid still has those feathers and headband.

Then we were ready for Kansas City, where some of the young cowboys went looking for that gal a guy had written the song about, "Kansas City Kitty," but I don't think they ever found her.

By this time, we had all the kinks and troubles worked out and had a very professional parade going. We were down to getting shaped up and on the streets almost on the minute, with everyone pulling together in a big team.

We were moving down the main street, Marg and I with our mules, when out of a barber shop raced this guy with the cloth around his neck and white lather on one side of his face, hollering my name at the top of his voice. We couldn't stop so we simply waved, and wonder who he was. When we got back to the station, I was being paged over the loudspeaker system, and was given a phone number. I called and it was a former guest, a hunter I'd had on an elk hunt a few years before. He had been having a shave and haircut when, through the barbershop window, he saw old Patches. He had just jumped out of the chair and ran out the door. "I knew you wouldn't be far away from Patches," he said. And was he surprised! He hadn't heard of our parading in Kansas City. And he never did tell me what the barber had said about his hasty exit from the chair.

We moved on to Louisville, Kentucky, where we made our first parade without freezing.

One of our former guests and her mother picked Marg and I up at the station and drove us to "Calumet Farms," home of Bull Lee, the world-famous racehorse and sire. It was great to see the magnificent animal, even though he was old at the time. You could see royalty showing in his actions and blood lines.

President Lyndon Johnson greets delegates from the Montana Centennial Train in the Rose Garden at the White House.

Then we went on to Frankfort, Kentucky, and up into the governor's office, where they made me an honorary "Kentucky Colonel," long Kentucky rifle and all. And, as we were leaving the room we met a group of dignitaries ushering in Montana's Governor Tim Babcock to accept the same honor. I have held it over poor Tim's head ever since — I was made a Kentucky Colonel before him. He was second choice.

Look out Washington, D.C., we thought, when we got to the nation's capitol, where we were really treated like royalty. The city came out and put on a big banquet in our honor. It was great. But before the banquet, a few things came up.

We paraded down Pennsylvania Avenue and around the circle at the White House. The sidewalks were lined with dignitaries; on the steps stood President Lyndon Johnson and others. Montana senators and representatives were right down at the street edge on the sidewalk, greeting us as each unit passed. When your unit came even with them, you simply paused for a minute to pay your respects to them.

When a unit would stop, out would step Senator Mike Mansfield, who reached out and shook hands and called everyone by his or her first name. Now, I was thinking that this old boy sure knew a lot of Montanans on a first name basis when I realized that the guy standing beside him had a paper and pen and was cuing him along with the names.

Right in front of Marg and I were Herb Toelke and the Tallyho. As Herb stopped his six-horse hitch, Mike stepped up on the loading step and shook Herb's hand, and said, "Good to see you again, Herb." Herb gathered up his lines and, with that big booming voice, said to his shotgun rider, "Who the hell was that S.O.B.? Never saw him before in my life."

As he drove away, you should have heard the people laugh, clear up to President Johnson. Herb was great but never ceased to open his mouth and stick his foot in.

The parade went swell. No trouble at all that day so everyone was ready for the banquet that night. With us were Bonnie Jo, Miss Montana, and Kitty Quigley, Miss Montana Centennial, who led the parade and appeared on television and radio stations, singing and answering questions about Montana. Now some gals just go along with the show, but not Kitty. You never knew what she'd do, but you could bet it would be different.

When we got settled down at our tables that evening in a huge banquet hall, Kitty was at our table. Dignitaries were giving their "One-two-three-testing" at the microphone and everybody was chatting, paying little attention to what was being said. Suddenly, a loud voice boomed out over the intercom, "Ladies and Gentlemen, the President of the United States." And in walked President Johnson, down a winding stairs to the podium. Everyone rose to their feet, but not before Kitty jumped up, gave a cowboy holler and jerked out her two six-shooters, which were loaded with blanks, and shot into the air. Now, you never saw so many Secret Service men in your life. They were all over Kitty immediately and had her guns — just about scared poor Kitty to death. The crowd went wild laughing and President Johnson thanked her for the Montana greeting, gave a short speech and left. I'll tell you what! Kitty sure put the cowboy trimmings on that high toned affair.

When we first started the real planning of this trip, Mr. Moses of the New York World Fair board offered us space for two years for our exhibit cars and asked us to lead the opening day parade to start the World's Fair of 1964, which we did. This, by itself, was quite an accomplishment but we also thought it was a great way to finish a month-long circle of parades and shows.

The Centennial Train exhibit was left in New York with a crew to tend it and we've never forgotten the volunteers who finished our big show in New York. A corral of poles was built and a few cattle were left to have on exhibit. One cow had a calf while New Yorkers, television men and women, newspapers and all watched and enjoyed nature from Montana at its best.

Then we were headed west, looking for mountains and home, and by this time you are wondering why this story is entitled "Patches, the Queen." Well, here it is. This mule, Patches, was a pinto, tall, well put

Marg and I talking with people at the World's Fair. Our stock waits patiently in the foreground.

together and had a character of her own. She could get into more trouble in five minutes than you could get her out of in an hour, but she was a good pack mule.

While we were on this tour, the Ralston Purina Company donated a horse ration to feed our stock. It was ground up alfalfa, corn, oats and barley compressed into pellets with molasses as binder, making it sweet and palatable. We fed no hay so the stock lacked bulk in their diet and they were always hungry and craved grass. When we were in Clarksville, Virginia, where there was grass between the tracks, we tied the horses on a line along the parlor cars to let them stay out in the fresh air during the night. One morning when we went to water and feed them, Patches was gone. How she got rid of her halter I'll never know. But, after a search around the train cars and puffing engines, we found the old gal across the yard, peacefully grazing between the tracks.

When we were at our last stop before heading home and were short on food for the horses, someone showed up with a truck-load of hay. We scattered it along the picket line so the stock could eat while they were tied to the line. The Shetlands were tied right next to my mules, all eating peacefully. Some kids, with their mothers watching close by, were sitting there, petting the Shetland's heads. One kid had a wooly head of hair, kind of a big Afro haircut. Well, he must have been in Patches' way because she just reached over took a mouthful of that pile of hair, gave the kid a shake and threw him out of the way.

Up jumped the kid, running toward his mother, screaming, "I was bitten by a mule." But that was as far as the incident went; the kid seemed to be pleased that old Patches had picked him instead of some other kid. As for Patches, she went right on munching that big bite of Afro hay. No pain, no strain.

On our way home, we got our first glimpse of those Crazy Mountains as we rolled into Billings, Montana, and we were anxious to be home. But the west-side-bound cars headed for Missoula were sidetracked and, after about three hours, a switch engine hooked up to the tail end of a slow freight headed west and we were once again on our way. We didn't get far when we realized that right in front of us was about five carloads of pigs. By then, we had lost our fancy parlor cars, so were riding with the baggage and the horse cars. Boy, you should have smelled the fresh air that came from the pig cars ahead. What a ride.

When we hit the Continental Divide out of Butte, those horses and mules started braying and whinnying and continued to do so until they were unloaded at the Missoula stockyards. How they knew they were home I don't know, but they did. We turned them loose in the stockyards and they started to run. And they ran and ran and ran, until each owner had loaded their stock on trucks, and headed home.

As for me, the memory of that trip lingers. It was a great trip with great people, many new friends and experiences no one else will ever have.

Thank you, Howard Kelsey, for dreaming. And Patches for some great memories.

(Editor's Note: This story originally appeared in the book "Copenhaver Country.")

Chapter Nine

Centennial Train Ride

$\mathbf{M}$issoula, January, 1964.

Herb Toelke, George Moore, Walt Vermadohl, Howie Fly and I were training stock to go on the Centennial Train advertising Montana throughout the eastern states, ending up opening the World's Fair in New York City. Mr. Moses, who was the head man at the fair, asked us to lead the parade on opening day and gave us a spot to build a huge pavilion which was to be run by the state of Montana for two years, as I remember.

We had everything that made Montana tick over the past one hundred years on display. On this train, we had cowboys and cowgirls, miners, ranchers, farmers, artists, entertainers, stagecoaches, a wagon train, Indians, over a million dollars in raw gold, copper, and silver ore. I had the pack string of mules and big game display. Packed on the mules was camp equipment, elk quarters, elk antlers, moose, sheep and mountain goats. In all, it surely was an impressive parade.

There were 306 people aboard, all paying their own way. We had young people in their late teens to old man David Cloyd Wampler who had come to Montana one hundred years before and also Molly McGuire, the first school teacher at Fort Benton and still a real fireball of a lady; also, world renowned Monty Montana and Stan Lynde. They

A group portrait of those on the Montana Centennial Train at Billings, Montana, in 1964.

were all grand people. In thirty days, I never heard an argument or any such thing and we lived on the train in close quarters. Everyone respected the other and helped out wherever they were able. I was proud to be one of them.

While in Missoula, training the stock to work in car and people traffic, we had forty head of horses and mules so we were on the streets every day. When these old ponies were brought into the fairgrounds at Missoula, most had never seen street lights or over two pickups in their lives. They all had long, shaggy coats of hair for winter, long manes and tails just off of winter pastures – really a pretty grubby sight. I must say, cars going both ways, honking horns and bright lights weren't in their bag.

We tried keeping them in box stalls with blankets on them but couldn't get them to shed a hair. No matter how much we washed, brushed, and combed their coats, they just wouldn't shed a hair. So, downtown we went and got some clippers and sheared them slick and clean. It was quite a tussle as electric clippers must have tickled them. We ended up throwing all of them and hog-tying their feet to get the job done. We put blankets on them at night, none in the daytime. At first, it was a job keeping the blankets on, but after they'd worn that blanket a night or two, they'd sure stand while you put it on, come the cold evening air of Montana winter.

It was only a few days and their hair was grown back so thick and about three-quarters of an inch long. They all looked ready for the president's ball.

While training, we sure had some great wrecks but nothing serious other than Freddie Deschamp's wagon. I must tell you about this one.

Herb on Ridge

Here we are in Baltimore, same old rush and run but were all lined up ready to go. Today we make a long parade ending up at the Baltimore Orioles ball park. Now to get in to the park we have to make a run down a hill under a viaduct, up a hill, make a sharp right hand turn, line up in a big circle around the diamond and give Montana pitcher to the Baltimore team. Governor Tim Babcock done the honors. The viaduct was only wide enough to leave four inches on each side of the wheels of the stagecoach and wagons. The street was cobblestone, uphill and very slick for the shod horses' feet. To make it you had to come down the entrance on a run and make this sharp turn at the top of their little hill and into the ball park. Now Old Herb is driving four head and you never seen so many sparks flying from shod hoofs on cobblestone in your life. Looked like fireworks at a Fourth of July party. He made it such a show of horsemanship I never saw before.

The Orioles beat the Yanks with the help of Dave McNally, our Montana pitcher.

Now on to New York and The World's Fair. What a show. We

were asked to open the fair by leading the parade with the Montana – It was great but I think the biggest Montana exhibit was when one of the Hereford cows had a calf in the pole corral. The crowd was big. They'd never seen anything like that before. At least, now, they know where beef comes from.

I'm just like a mule that forgot where the hole in the fence is at. Now in New York, we were camped at the Penn Station. After taking care of all the stock and getting the rigging cleaned up for the Parade next day, we headed for the washroom in the basement to clean up for the coming dinner. We ain't got much time. We're scrubbing our hands that are black from saddle soap and dirty leather when up walks this old grey-haired guy, "Here you guys try out my new soap. It'll really cut that grease."

Howie says, "Give me a bar. This damn hotel soap was made for washing dishes." He grabs a bar and sticks it under the hot water faucet and starts to rub his hands to make a good lather. Squeezing hard on the soap, "Bang" goes this bar and out runs the contents of a fresh egg.

Montana's Centennial Train delegation leads the parade into downtown Chicago.

Howie looks at his hands and spins around where our new friend is standing with a mind full of big long words. Flash goes the light, good and bright, and the guy smiles and says, "Smile, you're on Candid Camera."

Everyone was still laughing when we sat down to a great banquet, on time.

Now we're headed west and looking for white-capped mountains and home. It's been a long pack trip through a different world but great people.

Oh, I must tell you how horses senses work. About the times we were crossing the North Dakota line those horses started talking to each other and when we crossed the Continental Divide clear to Missoula, they kept it up.

At the stockyard in Missoula when we turned them loose in the pens they ran and bucked like a bunch of kids after being penned up all day at school. They knew Montana by the smell of the air.

Marg and I in Baltimore, Maryland.

After I got mine back to the ranch, they ran and chased each other for two days. They sensed or could smell the difference in the air me thinks. It was a great experience for all who went.

Finally comes the day we load everything on the train for the first leg to Billings to pick up the other half of the train people and stock. We have now a total of seventy-five horses and mules to be in the parades.

We are very well pleased with how our stock is handling the traffic and people. We have to be at the downtown depot at 8:00 sharp in the morning. This means we travel down Brooks Street to Higgins Avenue to the depot, right in rush hour while everyone is late getting to work. Didn't know so many people liked to work and all honking their horns and in a hurry. Wouldn't think so many people could be in such a hurry just to go to work.

Everything went well till Herb pulls his four-horse team and coach onto the Higgins Avenue bridge. It was full of cars going each way, looked like we had it made, only four more blocks. When out from behind a car, comes a guy on a bicycle, coat flapping in the wind straight at the lead team. He thinks he's going to pass between the cars and parade. Just like a flash, those leaders turned back, swinging all six across the road, filling the bridge. Herb is pulling on the reins, trying to straighten out his team. I believe every car on that bridge had two horns and the drivers were froze on them all.

In a minute, the outrider got hold of the leaders and straightened them out and away we went. Sure could have been a wreck if the outrider hadn't been on the ball. It sure proved why a top hand is so necessary with stock of any kind. We were finally loaded and on the way to Billings.

We pulled into Billings and unloaded our stock at the fairgrounds and go to breakfast. S'posed to put the whole shebang together, come afternoon. Us boys from the west side of ol' Montana only need forty-five minutes and we're ready to go. Six weeks of practice has done us some good. We find those guys and their stock ain't never done this before. You should have seen their stock and wagons; it was a mess. Those poor horses ain't seen no oats or curry comb for five months and some never before. Long-haired and caked with gumbo mud fresh off them gumbo flats and winter pasture.

"What we going to do?" says the big bosses. "We got three days before we pull out for Omaha."

I says, "Give us some men who know what to do and we'll shape them up." So a meeting was called and we got some good help.

Out came the foot ropes and clippers and upside down went the horses. Now by noon the next day, them old ponies was sheared slick and smooth; mane and tails trimmed, feet shod with borum plate shoes and ready for a run on the streets of Billings.

Wagon wheels were checked, welded, and greased, a touch of paint drying on the wagons. A few of them had their outfits ready to go. The biggest share of them were people who had saddle horses only, so the big job was cleaning things up to look sharp in a parade on the streets.

The next day, we paraded in Billings. Each outfit was given a spot in line and learned what to do. It was kind of a mess, but we had her shaped up by dark and ready to go.

Along that night about 8 o'clock, Howard Kelsey, who's the big boss on the whole deal, came to me and says, "We're short a saddle horse for Miss Montana to ride. She leads the parade."

I says, "I've got a couple of good ones at home but that's 300 miles from here."

He says, "How can we get one down here before tomorrow night?"

Me, I think mebby I can do it. I get on the phone and call Wendel, my brother, at the ranch and he agrees to load old Red and meet me in

Townsend, one-half way. Howard bums a pickup and horse trailer and I'm on the road. About 5 o'clock, we've got Miss Montana mounted and ready to go.

We're loading the stock on the cars when up drives this old guy with a big Palomino horse, unloads him, and says, "Where do I put him?" You've never seen such a dirty horse in your life. He must have been in a muddy feed lot with a bunch of cows all winter. He was long haired and shaggy, cockle burrs in his tail and mane. His tail, supposed to be white, drug on the ground. We loaded him and the old guy's gear, slammed the doors, turned the locks, and we're ready. Omaha, Nebraska, here we come!

I says to this old boy, "Ain't you ever curried the mud off this nag?" He says, "Never had no use for a curry or brush, all you got to do is wipe their backs with the saddle blanket before you throw the saddle on."

We rolled into Omaha, set up our display cars, polished up our gear, and cleaned up our stock, getting all set up for our first big parade at 10 o'clock next morning. Everybody was excited and lots of mistakes were made and corrected; sort of a mess. The deadline to be ready in your place in the parade was at 9:45. We made it! At 11 o'clock, we're still lined up and not moving. Horses and mules were restless and wouldn't stand much longer. There were no cops to lead us and open the streets with no traffic. Someone downtown forgot to assign patrol cars. At last, we're moving. Along with me, the stock have never seen so many people lining both sides of the streets over our five mile route. Everything went like clock work. People were great, gave us the right-of-way till we were back at the railroad station.

Oh, yeah, this old boy on his dirty horse would not stay in his place in line but ride over and shake hands with the crowd, holler and yell at people, ride this dirty old horse up and down the streets, never in time. Now, this old horse, dirty he may be but he was a dandy, prancing and throwing his head. He was a real beautiful and well-mannered horse under that idiot.

We jumped all over the old boy when we got back to the train. "Why don't you curry brush and clean that horse up?" We were ashamed to have such an unkept horse in the parade. He was a good horse, just needed care. The old boy says, "He ain't never had a curry on him, don't need it, won't make him work any better."

Now, us boys gets our heads together and decided. When Cal (the old boy's name) goes to the parlor car, we'll take care of old Dobie. Walt and Howie come out with foot ropes and clippers. Someone else hooked a garden hose onto the hydrant and upside down goes this nag. Now, if you walk through the railroad yards in Omaha today, you'll probably see Palomino hair blowing around in the yard. We sheared him, washed him down, dried off and trimmed his mane and tail. When we're done, he was a beautiful horse and he acted pleased.

Every rider took care of his own horse. He'd lead them up to the ramp of the car he was assigned to and us handlers would load them into their box stall, hang the saddles on the assigned rack. Everything had the same place throughout the thirty-day trip. In the daytime, we'd tie all stock outside to the hitch line and put them in the cars at night and feed them.

Along late in the evening, here comes old Cal looking for his horse. There is only three or four horses tied to the line. He looks them over and says, "Where's my horse?"

"Right there," says Howie.

"That ain't my horse!," he says

"Sure it is," says Walt, "look at his brand."

He walks around this horse and on the right hip is a big S/O. He never says a thing, just leads him over and we load him. Next morning, everyone is tying their horses outside and old Cal stands up on the ramp. In his big booming voice, he's telling bystanders, "Those dumb yokels never seen a curry or brush." "Look at my horse, he's clean as a whistle. They got no pride. I like things cleaned up." You never know about people.

Omaha, We're Here

You'll find that over 300 westerners got lost and poured out of those train cars. Pretty girls and ladies, Indian dancers, cowboys and ranchers, cowgirls and outfitters, farmers, and businessmen. The West was going east to show what our forefathers and mothers had found in the Big Sky Country.

They loved it. Train officials said between 800 and 1,000 visited the display cars while we were on parade. Governor Frank B. Morrison was honored guest that night at the banquet. The hospitality and food was great, just like old home day.

While we stuffed our faces and enjoyed the show, not a penny worth of that 1 million in gold or museum pieces were lost. We stayed till Tuesday night with solid lines of people going through the display cars and just talking and visiting. We were finding out there are no strangers if you open your arms and smile.

April 8

I left Frisco Kate hanging on the Golden Gate, when Kansas City Kitty smiled at me. Kansas City, we're here. We arrived in Kansas City at 4:30 on that cloudy misty day only 2 hours and 45 minutes to eat, unload stock and equipment, and line up for the parade at 8:50. "Can you guys do it? Watch us! We're old hands by now. We made the deadline in Omaha, didn't we?" This was a very long parade to a very enthusiastic crowd. People lined both sides of the streets cheering and greeting us; little people, old people, white people, black people, all wonderful people. No trouble, she went as smooth as silk. Must have been noon when we got back. We were sure hungry. Most of us horse people had no breakfast. The parade had to go first. After this, the head boss boys got the feeling, I think, that we had the show on the road. Didn't have no heavy push from that end again.

Teso Averill's poor old pony just couldn't take the confinement of the parlor cars. He was sick and crazy. We had to leave him in Kansas City. He was the only horse casualty we had. Claustrophobia, the vet called it. Whew, that's a big word for me.

We went to the Truman Library and had an interview with Harry himself. When it was winding down, Harry asked, "Are there any questions?" Now George Moore, an outfitter, stands up and in his slow drawling voice says, "Mr. President, have you ever driven a mule?" (George is a mule man.) Harry Truman says, "You're damn right, I've driven a mule. I rode one to school, too!"

The television, radio, and press were great, so many were on TV or radio. The Indian boys really danced it up on TV, giving us lots of publicity for cities ahead.

Banquet at the Sheraton Jefferson Hotel in honor of Governor Dalton. Entertainment "Montana Talent" from the Train.

April 10, 6:00 a.m. "Meet Me in St. Louie" We're here. Boy, what a night. That track from Kansas City was about like some of Montana roads. Either that, or all the wheels on the train were flat on one side. All night, it was pur, pur, ker, bump. Mebby two ker bumps and a pur, almost jolted your false teeth out but finally, we slid to a smooth stop in the Harry House Terminal. It was a rush, rush again for the parade but we made it. People were great and there were lots of them.

As we go down the street, Monty Montana and his wife, Joan, were riding along. Monty, as usual, spinning a rope around him and his horse. This rough looking ol' boy walked out from the street and grabbed Joanie by the leg. Monty just flipped that loop up and over Joan's horse, settling around this guy's neck, took a dolly on his saddle horn and jumped his horse forward, leading this boy down the street. You should have heard the crowd cheer. That sure put the big cure on rowdiness from then on. We heard the word went from city to city to stay out of reach of those cowboys and their ropes.

As we went up the street, I heard someone yelling my name, but I had to keep my pack string moving. I saw a man back behind run out of the crowd waving his arms. Seemed he had a white cloth around his shoulder and a white beard. After we got back from the parade and into the lobby, someone said to me, "They've been calling your name on the loudspeaker." I went to the office and sure enough, they had a phone number I was asked to call. I rang it and a voice I'll never forget says, "This is Doc Monday. Where can I meet you?" I told him, and shortly, in he came. Doc Monday was a hunter I'd guided in the Bob Marshall and also the Bitterroots, one great guy.

He told me this story and he was a story teller worth lots of

Monty Montana.

humor:

> *Now I'm sitting there in the barber chair getting a shave and haircut, when the barber says, "Look at that, must be that Montana Parade they talked about in last night's paper." I looked out the open door and I can't believe it. There's old Patches, your mule, walking up the street. I'm freshly lathered for a shave. I jumped out of the chair and out the door yelling to the barber. "That's Patches!" "If she's here, Howard's not far away." People think I'm nuts as I'm waving and hollering at you–this white cloth around my neck and one side of my face all shaving cream. "How about you and Marg come to dinner tonight?"*

Doc had a friend with him, Bob Sutherland, who owned a ranch out of St. Louie. He raised running and show Quarter horses. He said, "Why don't you come out to the ranch? We'll throw on some steaks on the grill and have a few drinks. We'd love to have you." Doc says, "OK, I'll pick you up at 5 o'clock. Then, Bob says, "What about those Indian boys, would they come? My kids would love to have them." Pat and Kenny Lefthand, Larry Park and Pascal Charlo, all Indian dancers, were delighted to go see these fine horses and fancy ranch.

There's one problem, Pascal has a problem with the giggle juice. So I tells him, "Now these are friends of mine and you take care, they'll be shoving drinks and you should make one last all night." "Don't worry, I'll do, I'll do."

We got there and looked the place over real nice. The boys put on a little dance for them and the kids, especially Pascal, got along great. Pascal was a great storyteller.

When they came with a before dinner drink, you talk about big glasses and I think they forgot any mix. I could see it was getting to my friend and then here comes another drink. I winked at Pascal to remind him of our deal, but he sips it real slow. Finally, the steaks are broiled and everybody was eating. I walked over to Pascal and he says, "How glad I was to see those steaks. I ain't used to such big drinks, all free. Didn't know if I was going to make it." Larry, who was in charge of the dancers said to him, "It's a good thing you did, or your scalp would have been hanging on their front porch."

The crowds were great going through the display cars and television, radio, and press kept many very busy. This was the historic part of the departure of river boats to Fort Benton years ago. Many of our grandparents made that river trip. Goodbye to civilization, they thought, not knowing we'd return some day.

We're looking for that Bluegrass Country, Louisville where the race horses are. Did we see race horses? Yes, and the world's greatest track sire, "Bull Lee", in his famous home, the Calumet Farms. I'll tell you about it later.

The parade went fine to a great crowd of very enthusiastic people. Here, I was asked how I kept the flies off those plastic elk quarters on my mules. Also had offers to sell them to people who wanted to taste elk meat. So, I figured Howie and I had made them very realistic. Here, we were met by Mrs. Bick, who was one of the big shots of the Democratic party in Kentucky, and her daughter, Betty, who had spent four years with us at the ranch and pack trips through the South Fork and China Wall country. By the way, she also suffered a broken arm trying to ride a steer while I was gone to town one day. She was truly one great gal. They rushed us off to their home and a tour of race horse farms and the home of the Kentucky Derby.

While at the Calumet Farms, we visited Bull Lee, a grand old stallion, who was grey haired on the cheeks and had a gimp to his walk. Father Time had taken a hold by now. But, when he stopped and raised his head, you could see royalty and fiery spirit of his youth in his eyes and poise. Citation and Whirlaway, his two fastest sons were stabled there, also – a great treat for a horse lover like me.

We rushed off to the capital of Kentucky, Frankfort, to be

honored by becoming "Kentucky Colonels" amongst the coonskin caps and long squirrel rifles of the past. As we were leaving, the door opens and in is ushered Montana governor Tim Babcock, Kelsey, Hume, and Bill Briscoe to receive the same honors. As we introduced our hosts, I made it clear that wherever we meet from now on, they should respect my rank of thirty minutes as senior Colonel.

After the tour of the Calumet distilleries, lipstick was given to the ladies and cigarette lighters to the man as souvenirs. "Nobody was even offered a drink," says Molly Sedgwick. "At least at Anheuser Busch they gave you a glass of brew." Right here, I've got to jump and tell you of Molly. She was a very gracious lady, one you fall in love with at the first meeting. How old, I do not know, but I'm sure she was smooth mouthed. She was one of the first school teachers in Fort Benton way back there in the late 1800s.

It was in 1965, Marg and I received an invitation from the Governor's office to attend a banquet in Helena honoring the people of education in Montana. We were pleased to attend. You could tell this was quite an affair, no place to park your car. After finding a spot, we were walking up to the entrance. A little old lady with canes came hobbling from the other direction. We met, and as we turned to the door, who was this lady, but Molly. Marg took one side and me, the other, and we helped her up the steps. Marg asked her where she wanted to sit in this big room. She says, "Up front." So, away we go. All three of us sat together, Marg on one side and me on the other. Sure didn't take long to figure this was a stiff-neck party as the lad who was Master of Ceremonies started his speech. (I even wore a suit and tie) He thanked everyone for coming and told us all it was in honor of the first and early school teachers of Montana. As he went along naming some of them he said he regretted that Molly was not here to help, regretting she was gone – intimating that Molly had passed on to greener pastures. Molly shuffled to her feet, waved her cane at him, and says loud and clear, "I ain't gone no place, by God! I'm right here!" People cheered and clapped and before she knew it, she was on the stage with the mike in her hand and the stiffness sure went out of the crowd. Don't know what happened to the first speaker, as we didn't see much of him the rest of the evening. Thank you, Dolly.

Governor Tim and Betty Babcock joined us, planning to be with us the rest of the trip through the World's Fair at New York, rounding out our Montana Family

Cincinnati, Ohio was a one day stop. We sure stuffed a lot into that bright sunshiny day. First, the parade in the morning. Walt Vermadahl had this six up of Shetland ponies hooked to a small Tallyho wagon loaded with kids mostly going for the ride. Everything went well until some wise guy decided to pass up the parade in his shiny Porsche. The streets were cobblestone and rough. As he passed up the Shetlands, off the Porsche flies a shiny hubcap, which rolled right up and under the ponies. Like lightning, those ponies were gone on a dead run. Walt pulled on the reins but those ponies were headed for the barn as they passed me and my mules. There was a clatter of hoofs and Monty Montana swinging a loop, caught them, roping the leaders. All was quieted down and the parade resumed. One casualty, Janet Schmidt sprained her ankle in the shuffle.

Now, back to Grand Central Station, the oldest and largest of all. As I recall, it was all wood. The lobby was huge, the woodwork was done with hand tools of many years ago. It made you stand in awe of the carpenters ability and desire to turn wood into something of beauty and durability. One whole side was restrooms with swinging doors marked "Men" and "Women".

All schools were invited to bring the children through the exhibit cars and view the Indian dancers on Monday afternoon. Here they came, a teacher in front and a string of kids thirty to fifty, then another teacher behind, marching in, row after row. I've never seen so many kids in my life – white kids, black kids, big kids, and small, so orderly and enthused. They claimed 2,000 went through the exhibit cars that afternoon.

The dancers had been to a television show that morning and as they danced in the front door chanting and ringing bells, all those feathered costumes, they met this string of kids, some leaving, some just coming. The lobby was full with them and train passengers.

Kenny Left Hand, who was always ready for fun, charged right into the middle of them, dancing, chanting, and waving his tomahawk. Those kids stampeded, shoving the teachers along. The only place of safety was the toilets. Those doors flew open and rooms filled with kids. Out came men buttoning their pants and women shaking down their dresses.

Out in the middle of the floor was Kenny. He'd caught this little Negro boy who was down on his knees, both hands under his chin, begging Kenny not to lift his scalp. Kenny picked him up, stuck a feather in his curly hair, hung some big bells around his neck, and showed him how to do a short dance along with the other dancers. I know that little boy, although a man today, still has a Montana feather and Kenny's bells. At least, I'd bet on it. Often, I've wondered what those poor teachers thought was going on.

I know the people who were interrupted in their chores, were laughing. One guy told me, "I got to go home and change pants," laughing as he went out the door.

On April 15th, we were in Bill Bolden's hometown, Charleston, West Virginia. Bill is our Train Manager. It was through him we bought ten of the railroad cars from West Virginia in the first place, then it grew to twenty-five cars. They were all brightly painted with murals on all external walls. There were pictures of Montana scenery, mining, timber, ranches, and farming.

Charleston is the home of many of my relatives as they filtered down from Plymouth Rock to Virginia long before the civil war. So, Bill Bolden figured Marg and I should see how many were dignitaries in the fair state of West Virginia. So, away we go to the courthouse to view their pictures hung on the walls. Many of them forgot to shave and had long whiskers and bald heads. Didn't make me feel any better, but enjoyed the tour of the city.

We rushed back for the parade and banquet, where Monty Montana and his horse performed on the stage at the Chamber of Commerce. Over 600 people enjoyed entertainment and a wonderful meal. It was one great city of wonderful people.

Hey, Mike Mansfield, shape up. Your constituents are in D.C. and looking for you. Boy, are we in a jam. That cotton pickin' train was four hours late and we have only forty-five minutes to be on the street and moving. We make it. This is the big one and we have to look good. We head for Capital Plaza, up Pennsylvania Avenue to the White Hour on Executive Avenue. We pass the front steps, lined with Senators and President Johnson standing in the middle of the steps. We pause a minute while Senator Mansfield steps up and welcomes each unit and President Johnson greets us. I'm telling you those politicians lose not a bet as each unit stopped, Mike would step up and shake your hand, greeting you by your first name and thanking you for coming. Sure had those names memorized. Never made a mistake. We had to cut the parade short by an hour and one half but everything clicked like a clock. The parade and exhibitor cars enjoyed a record breaking, enthusiastic crowd.

The Indian Dancers recaptured D.C. at Pershing Square. We finally had something to eat at Savarin Restaurant at 6 a.m. Boy, was I and the rest of the boys hungry. President Johnson greeted us Montana visitors in the White House Rose Garden where he was presented with a Charlie Russell picture by our group. Oh yeah, I forgot, as Monty Montana rode up to the steps of the White House, spinning his rope, he dropped the loop over Mike's head and led him down the steps to the edge of the street.

Friday was a rest day, with many just viewing different sights at the White House and surrounding historic shrines. The display cars did a thriving business again today. The banquet from 6 o'clock to 8 o'clock P.M. was in honor of the President and Congressman from Montana. David Brinkley and Chet Huntley were toastmasters.

Word got around that the President could not join us, but everything was going fine. Our train talent put on a great show. Chet Huntley and David Brinkley were doing a great job of entertaining the crowd.

At our table sat Miss Montana and Miss Centennial, Kitty Quigley. One never knew what Kitty would do, when on came the

Kathy Quigley (left) and Bonnie Jo Hunt during the Centennial Train delegation's visit to the White House in Washington, D.C.

loudspeakers, "The President of the United States" and down a long winding stairs came President Johnson and party. Like a flash, before anyone could stand, Kitty lets out a cowboy scream and jumps up firing two six guns in the air. Where they came from, I don't know, but we were surrounded by F.B.I. men who had Kitty pinned down and degunned – almost scared her to death. President Johnson took his place at the mike, and laughing, he greeted us all and gave a welcome speech. Festivities were great and it was the liveliest banquet of all.

An exciting development in the Montana Pavilion at the World's Fair was the birth of this calf, named Gold Nugget, to its Hereford mother, Sally. Celebrating the event area (from left) Paul Peterson, Ott Tschache, General Potter, Vice President of the New York World's Fair, and Bonnie Jo Robbins, Miss Montana Centennial.

Chapter Ten

New York

This old boy never was much of a city slicker, but I found out when Marg and I took a trip to Springfield, Massachusetts, in the later 50's that I could stand some learnin'.

We had an old Chrysler Airflow car and drove. I had an awful time with cars passing me at seventy or eighty miles an hour on a two lane highway. About the time we hit Minneapolis, I was doing all right and had my speed up to sixty-five miles per, sometimes seventy, just like the rest.

They were building a freeway through Minneapolis to Chicago, and that's where trouble started. The road was well signed right into the center of the city. There it stopped and every street I turned into said ONE WAY with arrows pointing straight at me. Finally, I got out of there after driving up and down every street in west Minneapolis.

I thought I had it made 'til I got to Chicago and got on the expressway going east toward New York. I never dreamed there was so many cars and trucks all going the same way at eighty miles an hour, eight lanes going each way and no place to hide.

We finally got off it and done good 'til we came to the George Washington Bridge in New York, and here were those signs again, ONE WAY, DO NOT ENTER, no place to go. I finally saw a hole in the traffic and pushed that Old Chrysler across four lanes and into one going across the bridge.

When we got across the bridge, the traffic was so thick I couldn't turn up the Parkway north so I mosied up a road that paralleled it, thinking there'd be a crossroad back to the freeway. No such luck. We got up on a little hill and I could look down and see the parkway and a sign pointing to Springfield, Massachusetts. Between us was a gentle slope down to the road. I swung that old car off the road and down the hill to the parkway. Well, when we got down there, there was a rock wall along the road about two-feet high. I drove up along the stone wall looking for a place to drive down into the barrow pit and back up on the parkway.

Pretty soon I saw a little shack with a light shining in the window up along this grassy-like meadow. I drove up and got out and knocked on the door. An old guy opened the door and you should have seen the look on his face when he saw me and my car parked in front of his door.

He yelled, "How the hell did you get here?"

I said I drove down from the road above and wanted to get on the parkway.

He kept yelling. "You're driving over dead people. This is a graveyard." He wouldn't tell me how to get out to the parkway – just, "You've driving over dead people."

I gave it up, got in the car and drove along 'til I found a place I could tear some rocks out of that wall and jumped the old Chrysler off into the barrow pit. When the traffic gave me a chance, I gunned that old girl and we were headed north on the parkway. Just like as if we had good sense.

Well, we finally got to Springfield and found that little rural town that Marg's relation lived in and figured we'd done great, no extra road expense. That old Chrysler ran like a dream. Now this was one of those old cars that had a soft top on it made out of a material like a raincoat. When we got up next morning, I looked out and there lies a damn goat right on top of my car. When I went out to chase him off, he couldn't move. All four feet had pushed through the roof and hung down inside the car.

We finally lifted him off the car and, I'm telling you, that roof was not moisture proof any longer. After driving all over Springfield, I found an upholstery outfit that could put a new top on it. It cost me $14.50. I'd hate to see the same bill today.

Well, we took another highway back to New York. Sure was pretty country, only too many people. When we got to New York, we came into a big circle sort of driveway where all the roads came together. Now, you were supposed to drive around this circle 'til you came to where your road turned off and scoot out right.

Well, I couldn't see any that didn't say DO NOT ENTER. Finally, I saw one and made a dive up it. I was doing fine, but had to drive between two streetcar tracks. All of a sudden Marg says, "That policeman is blowing his whistle at us, I think." By this time I saw we were following a streetcar and down in a big ditch.

That cop was running along the sidewalk up above blowing his whistle and waving his arms.

Marg rolled the window down and the cop hollered for us to turn up the next loading ramp where the people boarded the street cars. I did this and he was there to meet us and show us how to get back on the road. I couldn't get any directions out of him on how to get out of that fair city. He just kept telling me to go right now. I did and went the wrong way again.

Now, by this time we were looking for a dinner bucket and saw this sign, Greenwich Village Restaurant. I backed that old car over and pulled up in front.

When we got inside to eat, you wouldn't believe it only be seeing it. I had never seen so many strange characters all dressed different in my life, and hairdos that were unbelievable.

One character I'll never forget. She had what looked like her underwear on with this huge floor length fur coat and bare feet. You never saw such getups called clothes. When I asked people later about it, they would start to laugh and say, "Well, you can tell people you have been to Greenwich Village, New York." It sure beat Frisco at that.

(Editor's Note: This story originally appeared in Howard Copenhaver's book "More Tracks".)

Part Two

*O*ver the many years he toured the eastern states promoting his outfitting
business, Howard Copenhaver, as one of the most respected storytellers emanating
from the mountains of Montana, was constantly asked to share his tales with
audiences, large and small, in places like New York, Boston, Chicago, Cleveland,
Cincinnati, St. Louis, Minneapolis, Pittsburgh, and so-on. This led, in time, to
his transition from an oral storyteller to that of writer when he decided to put his
stories into book form, and his stories of certain incidents and episodes in his
adventurous life took on varied forms. Consistent with those he related from
place to place, however, were the five stories that follow in this part of "Mule
Tracks: The Last of The Story," stories of interesting characters, of mules and
mountains and grizzly bears that Howard considers among his best. While these
stories originally hit the public ear in his trips to the East, herein they are
excerpted from earlier books by Mr. Copenhaver, where they appeared in slightly
different form. They are used here because he felt they capture the essence of the
theme he's emphasized in this book, that of men and mules and wildlife in the
mountains of Montana, and in particular his beloved Bob Marshall Wilderness.
He wanted them to be a part of this collection of his stories, and we agreed. We
have acknowledged at the end of each excerpted story the book in which it
originally appeared and you can find dozens of other stories out of his beloved
mountains in his three other books, the best-selling "They Left Their Tracks,"
"More Tracks" and "Copenhaver Country."

Chapter Eleven

Ted, The Horse Trader

T ed was another character that worked for me. He was the best packer I have ever seen and could handle rough stock like nobody's business; the rougher the better for Ted. He was full of jokes. It never failed if things were really getting rough and tough, you could expect this Irishman to come up with, "Say did you ever hear about the guy..." and then he'd spin a yarn that would have everyone laughing and we'd forget our troubles.

He was always trading anything, but mostly horses. I'd be in need of some more stock and I'd call Ted and say, "Know where I can find this or that kind of a horse or mule?"

He'd say, "You bet. I'll be up with them in a few days." Or he'd say, "Come down and I'll show you some we can make a good deal on."

I always ended up with top stock at a reasonable price. Then he'd take my canners and trade them to someone else. He always had a deal going.

One day I called Ted up and said, "I've got these four saddle horses that are in good shape and gentle but just getting too many years on them. You know them." I told him their names. He knew all my horses, had worked them all.

He said, "This a trade deal or you just want to sell them?"

I says, "I'd trade, but later on next spring. If you want to come get them before the next sale, OK, and come spring we'll do some trading."

Well, Old Ted come up the morning of the horse sale in Missoula and picks up these four old nags. On the way to the sale he passes a bar. Well, Ted don't pass up many bars. He stops and is having a drink or two when in walks Old Barney, who owns Holland Lake Lodge. He says to Ted, "Where you taking Howard's horses?"

Ted says, "To the sale ring. You need four good gentle horses?"

Barney says, "Why's he selling them? They're good and fat and they're good saddle horses. I've rode them."

Now old Barney is ripe for a deal and the wheels are spinning in Ted's head. He buys Barney a drink and says, "If you want them horses, I'll make you a deal you can't pass up. You got any old canners up at the lodge?"

Barney says, "I've got three or four but there're not that good."

Ted says, "Let's go look at them." So off to Holland Lake goes Ted and Barney.

Barney has a little single-footing horse, but about thirty-three years old. He's the smoothest thing you ever rode. Then three other old nags. Well, Ted finally talks Barney out of $175 boot and trades him horses. Old Ted stops at the bar again and stays there 'til it's too late to make the sale. Hap, who owns the bar, says, "What you going to do with them horses?"

Ted says, "I'll take them up and dump them in Howard's pasture 'til the next sale." And away he goes, heading for my place.

Well, along about midnight Marg says, "Ted's here. I can hear him laughing." About that time the back door flies open and it's Ted alright. He's about half lit and laughing his head off.

I says, "Wait 'til I get this coffee going and tell me what's so funny." Well, we got our coffee and Marg, Ted and me are setting around the kitchen table. Old Ted starts in and tells us about his deal with Barney. Then as he's coming up the road below my place he meets Tom, who owns the Whitetail Ranch right next to our place. Tom stops him and says, "Where you going with the horses?"

Ted says, "I'm taking them up to Howard's."

Tom says, "Has he already bought them?"

Ted says, "He's never seen them."

Tom says, "How come you're always taking good horses to Howard and selling me some old canners?"

Ted says, "He pays me more money than you do."

Tom says, "Take them up to my place and we'll make a deal."

Ted says, "Fine." And up to Whitetail he goes, laughing all the way.

Now Tom had just bought three three-year-old half Morgan and Thoroughbred colts for $250 around, but didn't have anyone to break them to ride.

Well, after Ted and him had bartered back and forth for a couple of hours, Tom says, "Are they gentle?"

Ted says, "Sure." He opens the tailgate and unloads this little bay single-footing horse, jumps on him bareback with only the halter and rides him up and down the road. Now as he came by Helen, Tom's wife. he reaches down, picks her up on the horse. Ted slides off and Helen rides the horse down the road. When she comes back she says, "Tom I've got to have this horse. He's so smooth."

Well, Ted ends up trading all four of those old nags for the three colts plus another $175 and made a deal with Tom to keep the three colts for a month. Now Ted started out with four old canners worth $50 bucks apiece and ended up with three good young colts and $350 bucks to boot all in one day and had a party doing it.

I could write a book on his horse trading and trading for anything you can mention, even a gallon of paint on a billy goat. But that's another story.

Another time Ted was working for me and I had a very elderly gentleman on a special hunt. He wanted to get a bull elk on the bugle.

Now this old boy should have went on this kind of hunt thirty years before. He was not only too old, but in bad physical shape. One day I asked him why he never buttoned his fly on his pants. He says, "I can't. I've got arthritis in my hands so bad I can't pull the zipper." I said I'd do it for him.

Well, Ted traveled too fast for him, so I made a deal with Ted to cook and I'd guide the old boy. We traded jobs and the next morning me and hunter took off. We had not gone very far when a coyote shows up. He sets down on a hillside and is yapping at us as we rode by. I says, "You want to shoot that coyote?"

The old man says, "I sure would like to."

So I got him off his horse and all lined out. He let go and got the coyote dead center.

I told him to wait, I'd be right back. Then I rode over to the coyote and leaned down, picked him up and rode back to camp. I threw the coyote down in front of the cook tent and hollered at Ted, "When you've finished with your lady-like chores, skin this coyote out, Cookie," and rode off hunting again.

When me and my guest rode into camp that night, Old Ted hollers at me, "Hurry up. Supper is getting cold."

We went in to eat and sat down to steak, fried spuds, and onions and canned corn. I really like steak and fried spuds and onions and this steak was done just right. Nice and tender.

Now the hunt proceeded and all went well. We finally got a fair bull and the Old Man back to the ranch and on his way home.

Now along the next spring I was going to the horse sale in Missoula. I needed to pick up some new stock for the summer. My son or daughter said, "Think you'll see Ted today?"

I said, "I probably will. He usually makes all the horse sales. Why?"

By this time they and my wife are laughing 'til they can't talk. I finally wormed it out of them what was so funny. Now this damn Ted had steaked and fed me and the hunter that cockeyed coyote. You couldn't beat that guy with a club.

We had this party of men who had become very close. They all met the first time in our hunting camp. After that they made it a special deal they would come hunting at the same time every year. You talk about a rough crowd. There was Ted, Chuck, Bud and Lewie, all of them rough and tough. They would hit each other as hard as they could, wrestle and roughhouse like a bunch of kids.

Me, I'm small, usually about 115 pounds. They would pick me up and throw me right out of the tent. Then sometimes pound on my arms 'til they were black and blue. Never a dull moment. I'd wait and pull any dirty trick I could on them. This went on for years.

Finally, one night Bud came into our bunk tent and says, "Ted you got anything that'll help hemorrhoids?"

Ted says, "No. I got some Vaseline that might make them slick and they; won't hurt so much when you walk."

Well, this goes on for a coupe of days. Bud is in bad shape. He can't walk, sit or anything without pain. In the middle of the night, in comes Bud. He's got a flashlight and a shaving mirror. He says, "Ted where is that Vaseline?" Ted digs into his war bag and gets the jar, takes off the cap and sets it on the floor.

Now I sleep right next to Ted and I get a tube of Ben Gay (hot rub) and squirt a big gob of it into the top of that Vaseline jar. Old Bud squats down with the mirror under him, dips his fingers in the Vaseline jar, picking up all this Beg Gay and he rubs it on his hemorrhoids.

What a squall! Bud flies out of that tent, jumps in the creek, squats down and splashes cold ice water on his hemorrhoids, hollering, "Oh! Oh! Oh!" I'm laughing with my head under my sleeping bag.

After a while, in comes Bud. Now he jumps on Ted, who is laughing, and pounds the tar out of him, Ted yelling, "I didn't know it would burn."

I never told a soul, just let it ride. Now I really felt good because I'd gotten even with both of them.

Now these hunts went on for four or five years. Every year Ted and Bud would do battle the first night they met. I'm really enjoying this. Both thought it was the Vaseline. By the way, it cured Bud's piles; he never had them again.

Finally, he called and wanted to go mountain lion hunting with me in the middle of the winter. We were way up on a steep mountainside. The snow was deep and we were on snowshoes. Well, I've worn snowshoes all my life but Bud is having trouble walking. We sat down under a tree to eat our lunch. Bud says, "You seen that damn Ted lately?"

I says, "Yeah, I see him off and on."

Bud says, "That dirty son of a buck and his Vaseline, I could kill him."

I started to laugh. He looked at me and says, "Why, you dirty rotten little weasel, you put something in that jar."

By now I was on my way down the hill. Poor old Bud jumps up and after me he comes. He makes about two jumps on those snowshoes and end over end he goes.

I says, "Well, I cured your piles for you."

Bud says, "Yes you did but every time I comb my hair they hurt."

Now Old Bud and his lovely wife were really my kind of people. Both Ted and Bud have made the big trip over the Big Divide, but I really miss them as if they left us yesterday.

(Editor's Note: This story originally appeared in Howard Copenhaver's book "They Left Their Tracks".)

Chapter Twelve

Lady Luck Smiles

I walked into Trixi's one afternoon and up came this good-looking babe. She threw her arms around me and hollered, "Howard, it's been so long since I last saw you. This is wonderful." Everybody's looking at me and I'm sure enough dumbfounded. Then I see a smiling face grinning at me. It's Guy Clatterbuck, old Ted Clatterbuck's young son.

I said to the gal, "Mebby I should know you, but I don't. You look familiar but I see lots of pretty girls that look familiar. Mebby I'm just wishin'."

She said, "I'm Kay, Ted's oldest daughter. It's so good to see you."

Well we all chatted awhile and finally it came down to stories of long ago. Now Ted, her dad, was the best storyteller I've ever run into, so now I'm writing another one about "Ted the Horse Trader". This happened up at Ted's place just south of Ronan, Montana, on a sunny summer day.

Ted said, "Come with me. I want you to look at a real horse. He bucks a little they say, but has a rein on him just like silk. If I can buy him right I know where I can make some good money on him. Know just the right guy to sell him to. He's got a big ranch and needs good cow horses."

Now, at this time a $100 bill would buy just about any horse you wanted. You could get good geldings for $75.00. We headed for this old boy's ranch and Ted said, "I sure hope we get there before he rides this pony cause sometimes they won't buck after the first ride in the morning. This is the way it is with lots of spoiled ranch horses. Once they know you can ride them they just won't waste the effort till the next morning."

When we drove up, this old pony was standing in the corral munching hay. His back had wet spots on it and it sure hadn't rained last night, so we knew he'd been ridden that morning. But he sure enough was all horse; you could see at the first look. Had a lot of thoroughbred in him, sixteen hands tall, trimmed legged and 1,200 pounds of body on straight legs and feet, blood bay in color and a white strip down his face. He needed to have his tail and mane trimmed, but sure would turn the head of a good horseman anyplace.

Ted and this guy talked a bit and the guy said, "want to ride him?"

"Yeah, I'd sure like to," Ted said, as he hauled his saddle out of the truck. When he got the horse saddled, old Ted swung up and took a deep seat, kinda nudged the horse off center and headed for the gate.

Now that old pony let a squall out of him and went in the air, high and crooked. Ted was sitting up there looking good when all of a sudden they parted company and he stretched old Ted full length on the road, then headed back to the hay pile.

This guy went over, gathered the reins, and led the horse back to where Ted was trying to get some wind back in his lungs.

"Want to try another sittin'," he said to Ted. Ted was rubbing some spots that ain't needed rubbing before. He just grinned and said, "Sure."

This time, as he swung up, he kicked this old pony in the belly as hard as he could and rode off, not a buck in him, just plain good horse. You could spin him on his hind legs and what a stop! He'd turn left or right as smooth as silk. Ted stepped down and the horse trading began. This guy's been around some too. He finally got Ted to give him $175.00 for the horse.

The deal was all made and we loaded the horse in the pickup and headed south for this rancher's place, going down the main road to Missoula. We were driving along when Ted said "There's Bill right there." Ted turned off onto a dirt road where a guy was fixing some fence.

Ted said, "I got that saddle horse I was telling you about."

Now, Bill was 73 years old and pretty well used. You could see he was used to hard life and work. This guy looked at the horse in the pickup, then walked around and looked at this other side. You could tell he liked what he was looking at.

He said, "Well, unload him. You don't expect me to ride him in there do you?"

Ted jumped the horse out of the pickup, tightened the cinch and started to climb on him.

Bill said, "No I'll ride him myself." Like me, Ted was sure this was the wrong way to sell a horse like this one.

Well, the old boy swung up and so did the horse. Both were four feet in the air and doing their best. You could see this wasn't the first time Bill was ever on a bucking horse. He was doing a fine job but the horse won and laid him flat. He sure took out a big homestead in the middle of that road.

Ted ran down the road, caught the horse, kicked him in the belly and swung up and rode back to us, just as good as an old dog. He started to apologize to Bill, but Bill stopped him and said, "How much?"

"Six hundred fifty dollars," Ted said. "He's really a cow horse."

Bill said, "I'll take him."

Ted said, "You don't want him, Bill. You can't ride him."

Bill said, "I know and I ain't going to try. But I've got three young bucks working for me who think they can. This is going to be fun." And he paid Ted on the spot.

As we went down the road to dump the horse at Bill's place, Ted said, "That damn horse near killed me. I sure hit hard, but I'd do 'er again for $475.00 profit."

(Editor's Note: This story originally appeared in Howard Copenhaver's book "Copenhaver Country".)

Howard carrying the cape from Billy Lyons big billy taken on Danaher Mountain.

Chapter Thirteen

Walsh Party

After a letter or two over a few months, I get a phone call from a client. He and two other men want to book a goat only hunt for the following season.

Now, this is great, but he only wants one hunting license and wants to hunt nothing but a goat. His two friends are observers only. He's happy with paying full for all three of them, so this is good. Me and Gene, my brother, can handle them without help and Wendell and the other guides can handle the regular elk camp.

Now the day came and our guests arrive. One is an old man in his late 70's and the others are both doctors and young.

The next morning when we are making up the packs, here they come with their duffle. Boy, was it big, heavy and lots of it. We packed it up and lit out. We made our halfway camp in good shape, but a concerning thing was that Tom, the elderly gentleman, did not come to supper. The Doc said he was just tired.

Our goat camp was up Cabin Creek on the side of Scapegoat Mountain at about 8,000 feet. We were at our main hunting camp at 6,000 feet. When we started to pack up next morning, we suggested they leave all things not needed at base camp and only take enough stuff for overnight. But no deal. They had to take all their duffle. So what...It was only nine miles to goat camp.

Wendell Copenhaver with a Danaher Mountain billy.

We were camped in a meadow right at the foot of the last high ridge that formed the lower edge of this big basin on the top of the mountain we wanted to hunt. Scapegoat Mountain is a big, open, rocky mountain with lots of limestone cliffs and many wet cirques filled with succulent plants goat love to eat. It is the best goat country in Montana.

When we arrived at camp early in the afternoon, I was preparing supper when Gene says, "While you're getting something to eat, I'll run up on the bench and see if I can spot a good billy."

"OK," says I and away he goes.

He comes flying back in a few minutes and says, "There is about thirty head up there and a couple of good billies."

I dropped my supper, we got our hunter and says, "Let's go."

Now, from where we were camped to the bench and the goats it's not over 200 yards but pretty steep uphill on the main trail. Out of the bunk tent come our hunter and the two doctors. The doctors are carrying these two huge backpacks. They give one to Gene and one to me. "What's this junk?" I says.

"Oxygen bottle, hose, masks and medication," says Dr. Gray. Then we realize Tom is in really bad shape. Something's wrong.

Well, up the hill we start. All of a sudden, down falls Tom. The doctors grab our packs. Out come oxygen, masks, etc. They slap them on Tom and turn on the valves. Right away, Tom is ready to go again. Now this happened four times before we could peek over the rim into the rocky basin, but there stands Mr. Billy on a ledge all by himself. Gene got Tom into position and KerBoom, he's got his goat.

Gene says, "I'll skin the goat. You pack up and head for camp. We've got to get these guys out of this altitude."

"OK," says I.

When we got to camp, I put all three of them on their saddle horses and started them down the trail to the main camp. Then, I packed up their duffle, etc., loaded the mules and Gene and me caught them before they reached camp. The next morning, we loaded up and went out to the ranch.

Now I was a bit out of sorts at a man who would book a very strenuous hunt knowing he might drop dead at any minute and not tell his outfitter, so I jumped the Old Boy and told him how I felt.

His answer to me was, "If I had told you what shape I was in, you wouldn't have booked me. Now will you do me a last big favor?"

I said, "Yes." Then he gave me the cash price of having his billy mounted. Also, he gave me $100 bill to give the taxidermist to drop things and do his. Now $100 then was like $500 today.

In record time, the billy was done and shipped to Tom. Nothing more was heard for a long time. Then one day I got a hand-written letter from one of the doctors, thanking us for giving them a trip they really enjoyed. Then he went on to tell about Old Tom.

Well, Tom had hunted all over the world. He had a grand slam on sheep, lion, tiger, elephant, jaguar, etc.., from all over the world, but no mountain goat. He had reserved a spot on the wall in his North American Trophy room for the day when he got his billy.

Over the years, Tom had contracted leukemia and also bone cancer, along with about everything that could go wrong with his heart. Bill and Carl were his personal doctors and the went with him everywhere in his last years.

When his billy arrived, the three of them hung his head in the space on the wall. Tom sat in an easy chair admiring the trophy. Bill and Carl went into the bar and mixed a toddy to drink to the goat on the wall. When they returned to the trophy room, Old Tom, with a smile on his face, sat dead in the chair, the end of a life-long dream.

This makes you feel real good when you have helped someone gain a successful ending to such a dream. It's what keeps you going when you want to quit, just to be a part of fulfilling another's life.

(Editor's Note: This story originally appeared in Howard Copenhaver's book "They Left Their Tracks".)

Chapter Fourteen

A Disappointed Hunter

There was another guide who worked for me for a number of years. He was just a plumb good hand anywhere, but he had one distressing quality. He was deathly afraid of a grizzly. He claimed he wasn't. He called it respect. Be it respect or fear, he wanted no part of them in any way.

He was guiding this tough luck hunter for elk. The hunter had hunted elk over much of the elk country in the Northwest for fifteen years and had seen only one bull elk. In his words, "I saw one bull and stood there like a fool and watched him walk away."

Now Pat and the hunter were coming down along a creek late one afternoon when they came to a little meadow in the thick timber. Out in the middle is a big brown bump laying right in a spot of sunshine. The hunter says, "Is that a grizzly?"

"It sure as hell is," says Pat as he heads up a tree. Now Mr. Hunter lays it to the bear with that old 7-magnum three times. Mr. Grizzly just sort of flattens out on the ground, never even kicked. The hunter inspects the bear, shot three times through the neck. Pat says, "To hell with that bear. Let's go to camp." And to camp they came. We finally talked Pat and the hunter into going back next day just to see of the bear was still there.

Well, our hunter had done a good job and after much decision-making they skinned out the bear and brought the hide to camp. This was by far the largest grizzly I have ever taken in all my years in the hills. Clarence, the hunter, was hunting elk and that "cotton-pickin" bear was a waste of time as far as he was concerned. We tried to convince him that he had a trophy that any hunter would take above all if he had the chance.

To me, and I'm sure all outfitters will agree, in North America the Number One trophy is either a Grizzly or Rocky Mountain Bighorn Sheep. Here is a hunter who has accomplished this and shows his disappointment any way you look at it. To him, the whole trip was a complete failure. He is old and rheumatic and this is probably his last hunt.

When we got to the ranch (still no bull), I knew I had to do something or his disappointment would do me no good when he talked to his friends at home. We loaded all the elk and deer meat and heads and capes in the pickup with the duffle. I put this grizzly bear hide on top. We were going to Missoula to the taxidermist and freezer plant and then to the airport. Now I made sure Clarence rode with me.

When we reached the outskirts of the city, I stopped and spread this

A trophy he did not want. Howard and Clarence with a big grizzly.

bear hide out over the top of all the meat and duffle. It covered the whole pickup box and when I opened the tailgate the head hung to the ground. He was big! Then I drove slowly up the main drag and stopped right in front of the First National Bank. I says, "I'll be just a minute in here." When I came out there was such a crowd around that pickup I couldn't hardly get to it. Now, just as I'd hoped, right in the middle of them telling the story of how he got the bear was my hunter. Boy, was he steamed up and proud of that bear. I dropped off the hide at the taxidermist, gave instructions and made the airport on time.

A couple of months went by when we received this letter from the Old Boy's wife. She said, "Can't you get that taxidermist to ship that bear because if it is growing like Clarence's story, we'll have to build a new house when it arrives."

(Editor's Note: This story originally appeared in Howard Copenhaver's book "They Left Their Tracks".)

Grizzly trail, in the snow, across the Danaher Meadows. (Photo by Bill Browning)

Chapter Fifteen

Close Quarters

In September of 1948, me and my two brothers, Gene and Wendell, guided a party of six hunters from Cleveland, Ohio, into the mountains thirty miles from our home ranch on the Big Blackfoot, in western Montana. We were out for elk in the Bob Marshall Wilderness Area. We camped on Danaher Creek, at the head of the South Fork of the Flathead in prime game country. Snow had come early. The ground was patched with three or four inches, enough for tracking, and the prospects looked rosy.

Late the second afternoon one of the hunters killed a nice bull on Hay Creek, about two and a half miles above camp. It was decided that I would have the job of bringing the carcass home to camp the next morning. At daylight I saddled my horse and started out in the direction of the kill, leading two pack horses – a full-grown elk is too much for one. I didn't want to leave meat lying in the woods any longer than I could help on account of bears. An elk or deer left overnight is likely to be half eaten by morning.

The bears are more plentiful some years than others. That fall was a bad one for the beasts; they were hungrier than usual. The berry crop had failed and every bear in the mountains was on the prowl day and night hunting for anything that would fill an empty belly. So I wasn't surprised to see bear sign several times as I rode up along the creek.

Half an hour from camp I encountered a jackpine thicket that was too much for the horses, so I tied mine and went ahead on foot to find the elk and pick a trail for the horses up to it. I hadn't walked far when I crossed another fresh bear track, and the farther I went the more sign I saw. I started to hurry then, impatient to run off any bear and salvage what remained of the meat. But I was too late. When I got to the place where the bull had been dressed out I found only a few leavings and a broad, tell-tale trail where a bear had dragged the carcass.

I was mad. What guide wouldn't be if he had outfitted a party of guests, herded them on a hard day's ride back into the mountains with all their supplies and gear on pack animals, set up camp and spotted his hunters in first-class game country, only to have a thieving bear lug off the first kill? I had blood in my eye and just one idea in mind – to get back what was left of the elk and do it right away. And at the same time, I would teach the bear a good lesson.

I had hunted all my life and outfitted and guided for over twenty years. With that much hunting experience I should have taken a second look at the bear tracks before doing anything else. But in my anger I overlooked that little detail. The sign I had seen farther down the creek had been made by a black bear, and I took for granted this was one of the same breed. I knew it was big, for the elk would have dressed close to 400 pounds, but it didn't cross my mind that the bear might be a grizzly.

The trail was easy to follow. The bear had taken the elk up and around the side of the mountain, and it had made easy work of the carcass considering its weight. After 300 yards the track dropped into a series of deep washes and then angled up a steep slope toward an isolated stand of thick spruce. I knew I was getting warm. No bear would take an elk through there. The bear had headed for that thicket on purpose, seeking a good spot to stop and cash in on its night's work. I would find the bear in there somewhere, with what was left of the loot – which probably wouldn't be enough to pack out. I was getting madder by the minute.

I stopped at the edge of the timber and went down on one knee for a look-see. It didn't take long to find what I was looking for. I saw a patch of dark fur move behind a log, twenty-five feet up the hill, and then I made out the outline of an ear and saw an eye staring in my direction. The bear had seen me first.

The rifle I was carrying was light for the job. One day many years before, as a boy, I had shot a box of 8mm. shells at a coyote, which had been about 1,000 yards off, I hadn't killed the coyote. My shoulder had taken a pretty severe lacing, and as a result of that incident, I had developed the bad habit of flinching when firing any gun that slammed back at me. I had never been able to get over it, consequently I stayed away from the wallop packers. Most of the time I toted a .25-35 Winchester saddle gun.

I know it sounds screwy for a man in my business, but I prefer that little gun and do better with it. I knew a .25-35 really wasn't rifle enough for a big bear, even a black; however, I figured if I put the treatment in at the butt of an ear I wouldn't have any trouble. The ear was conveniently exposed over the log, and I was close enough that I couldn't miss. As I brought the rifle up, slow and easy, the bear came up too, fast and hard. It reared on its hind legs and let go a deafening roar that was enough to knock my hat off.

That roar told me, a little late, that I wasn't dealing with a black. I had walked into a grizzly as short-tempered as a stick of dynamite, and all of a sudden the little .25-35 seemed hardly more adequate than an airgun.

We looked each other over for mebby ten seconds, although to me it seemed like a quarter of an hour. I noted that the bear was a handsome old sorehead, with a dark, silver-tipped coat that shone like frost, even in the dim light under the spruces. I held the gun on the bear and waited for it to make the next move, hoping it wouldn't be in my direction. When the grizzly didn't move, I took a cautious step back, and then another. I kept backing up until I had a reasonable amount of yardage between him and the timber. The bear stayed put. I dropped down into one of the washes and then got out of there fast. I didn't intend to lead the pack horses back to camp unloaded, but knew I would have to kill the bear if I wanted to claim the elk.

I decided to come in from above and try for a shot in the open, at some6thjing more than twenty-five feet away. I made a big circle and worked warily down the hillside to the upper edge of the spruce thicket. I thought I knew exactly where I would find the bear. It would be on the elk or beside it, waiting. But I had figured wrong.

I was down on one knee again, trying to see under the branches, when the silver-tip cut loose with another roar so close behind me that I thought it must be looking over my shoulder. I spun around and stared the bear in the face. It was just six yards off.

It wasn't a pleasant sight. The grizzly was up on his hind feet like a man, eyes blazing, lips curled back and emitting a rumbling growl, the hair on its neck and shoulders all standing the wrong way. It looked twenty feet tall, and scared the hell out of me.

I had no chance of stopping the bear at that distance with the .25-35, and I knew it. No matter where I hit it, the bear would keep coming until it got me. There was only one thing to do; find a tree and, if I could reach one in time, climb. A grizzly can't follow a man up a tree.

It was slim chance. There was just one tree of the right size anywhere near, and it was between me and the bear. When the hunters paced it the next afternoon, they found I had been ten feet from the tree, the grizzly eight. I didn't have time to think. I must have acted from instinct, or from something I learned in the Navy – that a surprise offense is often the best defense. I yelled in the bear's face and jumped for the tree.

My yell must have startled the grizzly for a second or two as much as the bear's roar had startled me, and my head-long rush kept it off balance just long enough. I was already in the tree when the grizzly started for me and out of reach when it arrived.

When I started my dash I had my rifle with me, but when I reached a safe perch about twenty feet off the ground, I missed it. Looking down, I saw the rifle laying two or three feet from the base of the tree; the bear was smelling and cuffing at it. I realized later that no man could climb at the rate I had to and hang on to a rifle.

The grizzly blew its cork over my getaway. It danced around under me, bawling and raging and clawing bark, tearing up the ground like a baited bull. I was high enough in the tree to see the elk carcass in the spruce thicket, about twenty yards away, and I kept hoping the fresh meat would lure the bear off. Finally it did. The grizzly turned and lumbered down the hill, stopping every few steps to throw a warning growl back. When it reached the elk, it lay down beside the carcass. The bear, however, kept its head turned toward me.

The first thing I wanted to do was to get my rifle. I gave the bear a quarter of an hour to settle down and get interested again in the elk. Then, I started inching toward the ground, lowering myself from one branch to another.

I was careful to make no noise; the bear paid no attention until I was almost down. Then suddenly it seemed to sense what was going on. It lurched to its feet with a bawl of pure hate and came streaking up the hill. A bear can really cover ground for a short distance when it wants to. I went back up the tree a lot faster than I had slid down. The bear tramped around again under me for a while, grumbling and snarling, but finally made up its mind it couldn't reach me and went back to the elk.

I gave the grizzly time to lose interest once more, and then I tried another cat-footed descent. The same thing happened. The grizzly let me get down to the lowest branches; then it bounced up and came raging for me.

It's hard to believe, but the man and the bear kept that up for more than seven hours, from half past 8:00 in the morning until almost 4:00 in the afternoon. I lost track of how many times I went up and down the tree, but by late afternoon I was worn to a frazzle and realized that I couldn't keep at it much longer. Unless I succeeded in getting the rifle on the next try, I would have to give it up. And that would mean sitting in the tree and waiting for help to come from camp, a prospect I didn't relish. Gene and Wendell wouldn't start to look for me until dark, and I kept thinking how they would probably blunder into the grizzly then. I wanted to prevent that. But how?

Unexpectedly, however, the bear's attitude changed. It must have been getting just as tired of chasing me as I was getting tired of climbing. Or mebby it merely became resigned to the situation – it couldn't catch me in the tree, and I wasn't going to risk coming down on the ground. As I started down for my final try, the grizzly, lying on the elk, was growling and blustering and balefully watching me. When I reached the lowest branches, the grizzly stood up and bawled its resentment. But it seemed unwilling to be tricked into making any more runs up the hill, unless there was a fair chance of getting a crack at me. That gave me the opportunity I had been waiting for all day. When I had reached a point about my own height from the ground, I braced myself, legs tense and ready for a fast ascent. Cautiously I broke off a forked branch, reached out with it and raked the rifle up. I felt almost secure as I started back up the tree with the weapon in one hand.

But even before I was back on my perch, I knew I wasn't going to risk using my pea-shooter on the grizzly, after all. There was only the slimmest possibility that I could kill it with one shot, once it was hit and went off into the thick spruce, I wouldn't have a second chance. There was still Wendell and Gene to think about. If they came up along the creek after dark, hunting for me, the bear would be formidable enough. Wounded, it would be almost certain to kill one or both of them. Somehow I had to get out of this fix myself, while it was still daylight.   During the day, I had looked the hillside over countless times, but now I took another look and thought I saw a way of escape. As near as I could figure, it was about sixty feet down the hill to the elk carcass, where the bear was lying. Thirty feet the other way, up the hill, there was another tree I could climb. Beyond that one was a third and a fourth, each a little father apart. If I could make it to the first and then on to the others, by a series of dashes and climbs, mebby I could finally put enough distance between me and the grizzly so that the bear would stay with the elk and forget about me.

The first lap would be risky, but it was the only way to keep Gene and Wendell out of trouble. I would have thirty feet to cover while the bear was coming ninety feet. If I could get a running stat, I figured I could make it.

I let myself down to the lowest branches. The grizzly watched every move I made, growling ominously. It took all the nerve I had to let go and drop to the ground. But once I was sure the bear wasn't going to get up before I hit the ground, I did it. I lit running. I heard a gruff bawl as the grizzly lumbered to its feet, and could hear it pounding up the hill in pursuit, but my twenty-yard start was too much for the bear. I was safely up the second tree before the bear got there, and I had even managed to get my rifle up in the tree with me.

The bear was snorting and tearing around at the foot of the tree; then, after a few minutes, it gave up and went back to the elk. The next tree was about fifty feet farther up the hill. As soon as things quieted down, I dropped and went for it. It was duck soup this time. The silver-tip again came charging after me, but it had too far to run now to cause me any real concern. It took four trees, nevertheless, and a total gain of seventy-five yards before the bear called quits. It chased me up those four, one after the other. When I came down from the fourth tree, the bear paid no attention.

To make sure, I backed away a few yards, one step at a time. When I saw that the bear stayed put, I took off up the hill, watching it over my shoulder. I made a wide circle to get back to the horses, and then I started for camp.

It was dark when I rode in. I had expected my long absence to have caused some anxiety, but nobody showed any. Somewhat to my annoyance, my story provoked more amusement than sympathy. It took me a couple of hours to convince my brothers and the rest of the party that I wasn't just spinning a tall yarn. It was hard for them to believe that a bear would keep a man in a tree for a whole day. They finally were convinced that I wasn't kidding. Before turning in, the party had everything arranged for settling the grizzly's hash the first thing the next morning.

"If he's still there." somebody put in.

"He'll be there," I predicted grimly. "He won't move ten yards as long as there's a mouthful of that elk left. If we want him, we'll have to run him out."

The six hunters and three guides left camp at sunrise, following Hay Creek for a couple of miles and then riding straight up the mountain to get around the bear. I remembered an open ridge that gave a clear view of the creek bottom, the hillside and the spruce thicket. We planned to post the hunters along that ridge. Then Gene, Wendell and I would move down on the grizzly and flush it out. By following this plan there was no way for the grizzly to catch us with our pants down, as it had caught me the morning before. It was a good plan and it would have worked, except for one thing we hand' figured on. Nobody needed to go in the brush and flush that grizzly out. It was ready to come out without any prodding.

After tying the horses a safe distance back in the timber, we moved down to the ridge on foot. Most horses will bolt at even grizzly sign in a trail. We knew we would be asking for a big package of trouble if we tried to take them anywhere near the bear. We were bunched on the ridge 300 yards from the thicket, getting ready to send the hunters to their places. The bear was nowhere in sight. Then all of a sudden we heard a commotion on the hill below.

"Here he comes!" Gene yelled.

The grizzly had boiled out of the thicket and was plowing up the hill at a dead run, apparently hell-bent on tackling all nine of us. We let the bear come thirty or forty yards, waiting to see if it really intended to go through with it. Then, pulling up and standing on a fallen log, the grizzly reared high on its hind legs for a better look. We didn't wait any longer to see what the bear would do next, but we all agreed afterward that it would have kept coming if we hadn't killed it. The grizzly acted every bit as reckless and vindictive in the face of nine-to-one odds as it had the day before when it had put a lone man without a gun up a tree and kept him here for nearly eight hours.

Gene got in the first shot. He belted the bear in the shoulder with a 180-grain Core-lokt from his .30-06, and the grizzly dropped off the log with a bellow that shook the ground. But it didn't go down. It whipped around, bit at at its shoulder, pulled itself together and came pelting up the hill again, straight at us.

Then the mountain fell in on the bear! We were yelling and shooting and the horses were rearing and plunging. Three or four good solid hits were scored.

The bear kept its footing through the whole barrage, but seemed to be aware that it was licked. Still roaring defiance, it wheeled and started the other way as Wendell spiked it in the back of the head with a softnose. The grizzly was less than 100 yards from us when it went down.

When we skinned the bear we found it had copped nine hits, of which any one, given a little time, would have been fatal. The grizzly, however, had stayed on its feet until that final shot which had blown its brains apart. A bear that's aroused enough to attack man can absorb an amazing amount of lead.

"I was glad I hadn't tried for him with .25-35 the day before!" I confessed when it was all over.

We went back later to look over the sign and piece together how the bear had managed to surprise me the day before. It had come out of the thicket on the downhill side, picked up my tracks and trailed me as a hound

Howard Copenhaver with his .25-35 carbine and the grizzly that gave him the run.

trails a rabbit, following me while I circled to get above the thicket. It had stalked me with the stealth of a cat. The snow was frozen and crunchy, yet the grizzly had crept up to within eighteen feet of me – we paced the distance between my tracks and the bear's, and even measured it with a steel tape – without a whisper of a sound. Then it had stood up and bawled, ready for the final rush. Some hunters say an unwounded bear won't stalk a man, but that one certainly did.

The pelt squared nine feet, as beautiful a silver-tip skin as any of us had ever seen. They estimated its weight at not less than 800 pounds. Some of the eastern hunters, who had hunted Alaskan browns, thought the grizzly would go better than that. Whatever the bear weighed, it's a safe bet that no meaner a grizzly ever roamed the mountains of Montana.

Now as the old Latin saying goes: *"Montani semper liberi –* Mountaineers are always free."

(Editor's Note: This story originally appeared in Howard Copenhaver's book "They Left Their Tracks".)

Part Three

*W*hatever he did in the mountains, and almost wherever he went for

that matter, even places like New York City as we've learned, or Bishop, California, Howard Copenhaver was most often to be found in the company of mules. Some were beloved, like the legendary Patches and Black Moll. Others simply labored in anonymity, but they were nonetheless part of the saga Howard writes about in this book. Some of their stories also follow.

In this section, Howard pays additional tribute to two of his most prized mules, Patches and Black Moll. He also touches on the relationship several of these marvelous animals had to other persons with whom he shared the wilds of Montana's mountainous wilderness. And then, in a wonderfully sensitive story about outdoor ethics and the adjustments one makes to the vagaries of time he closes out his "last of the story" in powerful fashion.

One of Howard's best mules, Black Moll, is shown at the head of a string crossing the North Fork of the Blackfoot River sometime in the early 1950's.

Chapter Sixteen

Black Moll

Black Moll was a 1,200-pound beautiful half-Thoroughbred Morgan-cross mare. Black as night, with a white star in the forehead and white snip on the nose. She had all the beautiful things a man wants in a saddle animal: small head, well-rounded body, trim legs and a spirit to match it all.

She was a three-year-old when we started to ride her. She didn't offer to buck, not once, but the minute you pried her off center she'd stampede, run blind and she could run. You couldn't stop her or control her in any way.

My brother gets on her once day and away she goes, right through the corral fence. He bails off and says, mixed with other words, "Let's shoot her and feed her to the hounds." I fully agreed as I'd taken some hair-raising rides on her, too.

Well, about the next day or so up drives Peter Genoff, a neighbor, and wants me to pack a bull elk off the mountain above the ranch. I finally agreed to help him the next morning.

Well, I had two saddle horses in the corral and this black mare. Pete didn't want a saddle horse, said he'd rather walk. I says, "I'm going to take that black witch and pack her." Wendell sais, "You're only asking for trouble." Me, I says, "If I can't pack her, I'll kill her."

Well, Pete couldn't find his way to the elk. Seemed like I followed him all over Bull Mountain, but about four in the afternoon we found his elk.

We cut it up into four quarters and were ready to load up. I tied that nag to a solid tree and tied up her hind foot. After some time, I got her loaded. It was a big bull, so each quarter weighed about 125 pounds apiece. I loaded the other horse and since it's getting close to dark, I lead my lead horse over to Moll and untied her from the tree.

Like a flash, she whirled and jerked away. Down the hill she goes. I can hear her crashing for a long time, then all is quiet so I tied up my stock and down the hill goes me and Pete looking for this crazy mare. Finally, way down the hill I hear a log snap and then a big crash. I holler at Pete and says, "She's made it to the bottom. I'm going after my saddle horse and pack animals and I'll meet you on the road somewhere."

Well, by the time I reached the end of the road at the bottom, it's just as dark as the inside of a cow. Pete hears me coming and hollers, so we're together again – but no black mare.

I says, " I'll look her up in the morning. At least we have the head and the hind quarters. Let's find the house and something to eat." Now we cross the meadow to the lights of the house.

When we get just about to the gate, there lays that old black heifer on the ground. Her saddle has turned with one quarter under her belly and one on top, with her feet tangled in all the ropes. I'll tell you, she is well anchored.

We got her all untangled and on her feet. She looks like someone has given her a shampoo and forgot to wash the soap off. We load her again, only this time we didn't need any foot rope. She's had enough for one day, and so have me and Pete.

Now swallow this. We used that mare for a bell mare with the mules till she was twenty-five years old and she never was anything but gentle and honest, from that time on out.

Chapter Twelve

Patches

One day on the upper reaches of Sheight Creek up in the Bitterroots, my hunter shot a big ole bull elk on a steep mountain side. This side of the mountain was tall bunch grass covered with about six inches of snow. When the elk fell he started to slide down the hill. All you could see was a big cloud of snow in the air, I know I was in trouble because just below this gassy hillside was a rocky canyon above the creek. I believed it impossible to get pack stock in there. The elk slid, in all, at least 1,000 feet or more before coming to a halt against a big old log near the creek.

I went down and dressed him out and finally found a way I could get my mules to him by working them slow from one rock ledge to another but getting back out with a load was another thing.

Next day one of my guides went with me and we took these mules to lighten the loads. Rhubarb, Raisin and Ole Patches, a long legged pinto mule. We took them down one at a time. After we had them loaded, we started back up the steep rocky side, I couldn't climb fast enough to keep out of old Patches way, so I says to Smoke, "Tie up Raisin's halter rope and turn her loose." I did the same to Ricky and Patches, them stepped out of the way and said, "Go home."

Away goes Patches up the ledge, the other two right behind her. Now she missed the trail we'd come down and found herself on a ledge where she was up against a cliff and could not go any farther. Both other mules right behind her. All three out on this narrow ledge, no place to turn around.

They stood there for a while. Smokie and me wondering what to do as we couldn't go get them. Finally Raisin started to back up, both other mules put it in reverse. When he came to a spot they could turn around, he stopped and let Patches get by. She smelled the ground and took up the mountain, Ruby and Raisin right behind her.

Smokie and me right after them only not as fast. When we got up on top where we left our saddle horses, all three of those hard tails were standing there with a look on their faces that said very plain,

"Where you guys been?"

This illustration by Anthony Lapka relates to the story on Page 38 in which Howard recommends that you never turn stock loose with a halter left on them.

Chapter Eighteen

Bishop, California, Mule Days

Now we're talking about mules. Marg and I drove down to Bishop, California, one year to watch their big celebration known as "Mule Days." What a great show and such good mules!

These were not the type of critters we like for pack mules. Just too much hot blood, causing too light of both muscle and bone. But beautiful saddle stock. I would say their dames were either Thoroughbred or quarter mares. Real nice but still full of mule brains. And thinking.

One evening we were watching the races. There were some fast, hard tails in those races. I mean they could sure cover a lot of ground in a short time. I believe it was a quarter of a mile track, fenced all the way around except for about 150 feet just before the finish line. Here they had a rope straight across the opening of the arena where they had the jumps set up for the next day's events. Well, now, these old long-ears are sure raising a dust coming up the home stretch, one little mule three lengths ahead and sure picking them up and laying them down. The crowd is wild cheering her on.

When she reached the space where the rope was stretched, her old ears came alive. As she came up the track, they'd keep bending over toward that rope with the ribbons hanging down from it, to make it look like a fence. Me, I says to Marg, "Watch that mule, she's going under that rope." Sure enough, when she got about halfway to the finish line, down went her head and she dove under that rope. Her poor jockey (a little gal) didn't make the dive. That rope took her about belt high and stretched her out flat on the track.

Now long-ears just trotted out in the areana bout fifty feet and stopped, turned around as if to say "I'm sorry." The little lady was helped up and when she got her air (no first place), hobbled out there, picked up the reins and walked off the arena, this beautiful little hard-tail following along behind like nothing had happened.

The next day was the big day of the show. They had this deal where you rode a series of jumps over bars and ditches, all sorts of obstacles. I think they called it a steeplechase. How those mules handled those jumps was a sight to see. Next came the high jump and this one guy on a slim, black mule broke the world record for height – somewhere like six feet one inches. The following day he was going to try to break his own world record. They set the pole at five and one-half feet to start and he cleared it just like nobody's business. They raised the bar to six feet one inch and again he made it with inches to spare. The crowd was just hysterical with applause, so up goes the bar another inch.

Down the track comes this long-ears and rider. Mr. Donk has his lead just right and you know a record is about to be broken in his last, long stride before the jump. On comes the brakes, all four of them! Mr. Rider goes over his head and slides under the bar. He get up and takes another run at the jump. When long-ears comes to the bar, it's a sudden stop again! The rider picks up his reins and takes his bows. Then he starts to lead his mule around the end of the jump. But no! This old hard-tail has decided different. He jerks away from the rider, spins around and clear s that jump by a foot. Then, with head high and tail in the area, he heads across the arena for the stable with the rider limping along behind.

Who's got a mind of his own? The rider or the mule? The crowd is wild, and I'm sure they're cheering the mule. I love those long-ears.

Chapter Nineteen

Lady and Glory

You'd think I just plain hated horses. Not so! I've had some of the best horses a man could ever want. True as gold and a lot cheaper.

I must tell you about two such nags. Lady was a raw-boned, part Thoroughbred mare, bay in color. Glory was a Palamino of mixed breeding. Both were top saddle animals but when we were in rough, tough country packing out a bull elk and needed trustworthy stock these two got the job done. I always said if a man can walk in there and out, Lady and Glory can do it with a load on their backs and you can't keep up.

Many is the time I've taken these two into some tough hole, loaded them with two elk quarters apiece, tied the antlers on top and turned them loose. They'd head off that mountain straight for camp, right up to the cook tent and stop. The cook would unload them and turn them loose.

Then they'd go out to graze with the other stock, and never stop to graze on the way. Meanwhile, me and my hunter would go on hunting back to camp.

This went on for a number of years. Finally, I hired a big German kid who had a mind of his but a better man you couldn't find. One of my guides and his hunter shot a huge bull elk up on Jumbo Mountain one evening. When the bull rolled down into a deep wash by a little stream, a tough piece of real estate, Howard, the guide, said he'd go get the elk in the morning.

I told him to take Lady and Glory, as the hunter was going with him. I said, "You guys pack the meat up out of that wash before you pack those horses, and be sure you're in fair country before you put the antlers on top." They said, "Okay, we'll be fine."

Well, when they got there Howard found a spot he could just lead those two horses right down to the elk. After mantying up the meat in canvas and loading it on, he loaded this big six-point head on top and tied it down right, then took the lead rope and up the bank he went. When Lady came to the top she had to give a little jump over the edge to solid ground. The bank gave way and over backwards she went, back into the ravine. As she hit the bottom, her head flew back and ran a tine of those antlers into her neck. This was a quick way out but not nice.

When I got to camp that night, Howard and the hunter wee sitting out by the corral crying. I felt a lot sorrier for them than losing a top horse. It sure proved to them and everyone else in camp – don't take chances in the mountains, even if it looks faster and easier. I sure missed that old bay mare for many years.

Chapter Twenty

Dodge City

I don't recollect jut where he came from. I think he was a real small-jack mule in a carload I bought from a dealer from Missouri or Kansas.

This guy came to Missoula with thirty head of mules, planning on selling them at the auction ring. When he got there the owner wouldn't allow him to unload them. Plus, the railroad was charging him demurrage and he was losing money every day.

Someone told him to call me, that I needed mules. Well, I really didn't at the time. But he talked me into buying them at $125.00 per head and holding them and selling them as I could. Well, I didn't make any money on them but got a lot of use out of the bunch and kept the best for myself.

This one little jack sort of crawled into my heart and I called him "Dodge City." He didn't weigh over 900 pounds but had fire and was a well-reined saddle mule.

I don't like a saddle mule but my guests sure did, especially those with short legs. Dodge City was only fifteen hands tall and traveled real smooth and easy, very gentle, nothing but manners. Seemed to love people and their petting and patting him.

We had an elderly, short and fat Supreme Court judge who always came for a large trail ride. After the first ride on Dodge City, he wouldn't ride anything else.

Chapter Twenty-one

The Phantom Hunter

O ne fine day late in the season, I found myself and a guest high on the southwest side of Sugarloaf Mountain hoping to catch and old bull elk on his way to the winter range on the headwaters of the Sun River.

This was one of the main migration trails to and from the South Fork of the Flathead Country to the Sun River Game Range. We were sitting on an outcropping, rocky cliff looking across the head of Rapid Creek right into the south face of Sugarloaf Mountain.

There was a deep draw running down, racing us and the game trail that led to the Sun River Country. Snow covered most of the ground to a depth of three or four inches. Some spots were bare, but this draw was deep and filled with snow. We were watching five or six mountain goats feeding on a bare spot near the top when, all of a sudden, they took off on a run straight at this snow-filled draw.

Watching them with our glasses, we saw two mountain lions running after them on each side, Plainly herding them into the draw and the deep snow. They all disappeared over the edge. Soon five goats climbed out on the opposite bank and ran up the cliffs. We watched and soon a lion dragged the sixth one back out on our side of the draw to open ground. The second cat soon joined his buddy and supper was served. What a sight for some hunters that didn't know the score.

Gathering the stock. That's Patches in the lead at the back of the photo.

Chapter Twenty-two

Dillinger

O h yes, and then there was a long-ears called Dillinger. What a character.

You could ride your tail off wrangling in the frosty morning and never get a sight of this guy. So, you give up and gather the rest of the stock and head for camp, get them all caught and saddled, ready to pack and sometimes be half loaded when you'd see a mule's head peeking around a tree out there a ways.

So you'd just go ahead and keep packing and pretty soon up walks Ole Dillinger and stand in his place by the other mules. Then you'd pick up his halter and rigging, walk over and saddle and halter him, load him and tie him in his place and he's ready for a good day's work. Don't know how come he started doing that, but that's the way it was.

A break along the trail on misty mountain morning.

Chapter Twenty-three

The Road Hunter

Long before I was old enough to hunt on my own, I grew to despise spotlighters and people who drove up and down the road and shot deer and elk from their cars. They were called road hunters and a few other choice names not used in mixed crowds.

Some were understandably back then as they are today. Today, with so many roads through the game country, it is the only way you can get to your choice area. I was a believer of fair chase only. A hunter who shot game over the fence in someone's meadow was a bum or an old boy who shouldn't have been hunting anyway.

To me, a sportsman was a guy who made it to the craggy tops on foot and outsmarted a big mossy horned buck or bull elk in his own country; the game using four legs, and you, two. Outmaneuvering and outguessing him on wind currents, having better, faster eyes. Fighting snow and dead fall timber both in getting to him and packing out the meat and trophy heads.

If you could walk faster come night than one half mile an hour, you sure hadn't put in a day's hunt. A real hunter would never hunt the flat land close to the road. He should hunt the highest ridges and roughest country just to make it fair chase.

I remember well one very successful hunt in the back country. We had eight hunters and everyone got a bull elk and also several mule deer bucks. When we hit the corrals at the end of the road and were unpacking the mules, up the road came this new pickup truck.

In this pickup, was a driver and passenger. Both had rifles across their laps with the barrels sticking out the windows. In the back were three more guys sitting on bar stools fastened to the pickup floor. Each had a padded bar in front of them as a gun rest. In the back was an empty bar stool.

They stopped, admired our heads and talked to my hunters. One said, "We've driven 300 miles today and never got a shot." As they drove off, old Larry Kollar yelled and stopped them. Then, he hollers, "You guys travel too fast, you've lost your tail gunner." No answer, just the roar of the motor and the spinning of the wheels throwing gravel.

In the Danaher, they started packing and setting up a sort of camp. Riding up and down the trail lots of times at a trot or a lope. No one can shoot an elk from a horse on the trail at that speed. All they did was drive the game to rougher country. They'd stop at my camp for coffee and friendly visit on the way in. Three or four days later, I saw them headed out, usually on a trot, packs flopping up and down their pack animals. Not a smile or wave as they went by. Later, the Forest Service Ranger would come by or write us of the complaints they'd received of the things us, as outfitters, were doing wrong and ruining the country and killing all the game; unjustly giving us outfitters a bad name and trouble we'd have to iron out.

As years went by, I noticed I didn't get to the top ridges anymore. Seemed like the more gentle ground at a slower pace looked better to me. Mebby I didn't see as much country or game, but we got game, only it took more time. Funny, but my guests seemed to not get so tired.

I've had a few more birthdays and those mountains just higher and downfalls thicker and higher. Then, the mountains grew steeper and thicker and I couldn't make it.

One day, I took the pickup and just drove up some logging roads and found a vantage point. Toby, my dog, and I descended to just look at the beautiful view down the valley and the tops of those high ridges I couldn't get to.

Old Toby and I just sat there never saying a word. I think we knew what was on each other's mind. Toby had been with me since a weaned pup and we'd traveled many miles of mountains and trails together over the last twelve years.

All of a sudden, Toby sticks his nose out the window and looks back behind the truck. A soft growl comes from his throat. I take a quick look and down the mountain behind us comes this beautiful five-point buck. I gently opened my door and slipped out, taking my rifle with me. I stepped away from the truck and got a clear shot. Down comes the buck and out the window flies Toby, right to the buck. Toby grabs him by the neck and starts dragging him. It's really steep ground and there's a road bank right behind the pickup. I backed the pickup up against the bank, opened the tailgate, and together, Toby and I dragged him onto the tailgate. I forgot to tell you, I'd gotten hurt in the hills a while before and flew out to the ranch by helicopter, so I couldn't do much except on my knees.

This was my first experience at road hunting. As the mountains have gotten taller and birthdays more often, I've taken a different look at road hunting and people that do it. We're not such bad guys after all. Just as long as it's fair chase and not on a highway or with a spotlight, and by permission of land owners. If I didn't do it this way, I'd have given up hunting five or six years ago. You don't run races at eighty-six years young and you can take some young fry with you and teach him many things about the woods and wilds.

Funny how time changes everything. You know the only thing that doesn't change is the beauty and solitude a man gets by himself out there. Where a man has nothing to do with it all, the towering trees, tall grass, the sound of a rushing stream, majestic peaks topped by a clear blue sky that we sure can't change. God's Country all for us Old Jokers.

LISTING OF BOOKS

Additional copies of *MULE TRACKS: THE LAST OF THE STORY* and many other of Stoneydale Press' books on outdoor recreation, big game hunting, or historical reminisces centered around the Northern Rocky Mountain region, are available at many book stores and sporting goods stores, or direct from Stoneydale Press. If you'd like more information, you can contact us by calling a Toll Free Number, **1-800-735-7006**, by writing the address at the bottom of the page, or contacting us on the Web at www.stoneydale.com. Here's a partial listing of some of the books that are available, including a grouping of Howard Copenhaver's popular books.

Books By Howard Copenhaver

Copenhaver Country, By Howard Copenhaver, the latest collection of humorous stories. Contains rich humor and studied observations of a land Howard loves and the people he met along the way in a lifetime spent in the wilds. 160 pages, many photographs. Hardcover and softcover editions.

They Left Their Tracks, By Howard Copenhaver, Recollections of Sixty Years as a Wilderness Outfitter, 192 pages, hardcover or softcover editions (One of our all-time most popular books.)

More Tracks, By Howard Copenhaver, 78 Years of Mountains, People & Happiness, 180 pages, hardcover or softcover editions.

Historical Reminisces

Indian Trails & Grizzly Tales, By Bud Cheff Sr., 212 pages, available in clothbound and softcover editions.

70,000 Miles Horseback In The Wilds of Idaho, By Don Habel. Don Habel worked as an outfitter in the Idaho wilderness for more than forty years and has put together a wonderfully detailed and sensitive, as well as occasionally humorous, reminisce of his adventures in the wilds. 180 pages, softcover.

The Potts' Factor Versus Murphy's Law, By Stan Potts. Life story of famous Idaho outfitter Stan Potts, lots of photographs. 192 pages.

Mules & Mountains, By Margie E. Hahn, the story of Walt Hahn, Forest Service Packer, 164 pages, clothbound or softcover editions.

Dreams Across The Divide: Stories of the Montana Pioneers, Edited by Linda Wostrel, Foreword by Stephen Ambrose. Stories and photos of the first pioneers to settle in Montana. 448 pages.

Another Man's Gold: A Novel of the Life & Times of James B. Stuart in Early Montana, By Rod Johnson. Cattle drives, gold panning, rustlers, hangings, battles with outlaws feature this story of one of Montana's first settlers.

STONEYDALE PRESS PUBLISHING COMPANY

523 Main Street • Box 188
Stevensville, Montana 59870
Phone: 406-777-2729
Website: www.stoneydale.com